Dating After 50

This Large Print Book carries the
Seal of Approval of N.A.V.H.

Dating After 50

*Negotiating the Minefields
of Midlife Romance*

Sharon Romm, MD

Thorndike Press • Waterville, Maine

Published in 2005 by arrangement with Quill Driver Books/Word Dancer Press, Inc.

Thorndike Press® Large Print Senior Lifestyles.

The tree indicium is a trademark of Thorndike Press.

The text of this Large Print edition is unabridged.
Other aspects of the book may vary from the original edition.

Set in 16 pt. Plantin by Ramona Watson.

Printed in the United States on permanent paper.

Library of Congress Cataloging-in-Publication Data

Romm, Sharon.
    Dating after 50 : negotiating the minefields of midlife romance / by Sharon Romm.
        p. cm.
    Originally published: Sanger, Calif. : Quill Driver Books, c2005.
    Includes bibliographical references.
    ISBN 0-7862-7866-8 (lg. print : hc : alk. paper)
    1. Dating (Social customs)   2. Middle aged persons.
3. Man-woman relationships.   4. Large type books.   I. Title.
HQ801.R646 2005
    646.7′7′0844—dc22   2005012825

Dating After 50

As the Founder/CEO of NAVH, the only national health agency solely devoted to those who, although not totally blind, have an eye disease which could lead to serious visual impairment, I am pleased to recognize Thorndike Press★ as one of the leading publishers in the large print field.

Founded in 1954 in San Francisco to prepare large print textbooks for partially seeing children, NAVH became the pioneer and standard setting agency in the preparation of large type.

Today, those publishers who meet our standards carry the prestigious "Seal of Approval" indicating high quality large print. We are delighted that Thorndike Press is one of the publishers whose titles meet these standards. We are also pleased to recognize the significant contribution Thorndike Press is making in this important and growing field.

Lorraine H. Marchi, L.H.D.
Founder/CEO
NAVH

★ Thorndike Press encompasses the following imprints: Thorndike, Wheeler, Walker and Large Print Press.

Contents

Introduction

After years of unsatisfying relationships, I took a five-year break from the miseries, anxieties, and fleeting pleasures of dating. Those years were productive and happy ones. I didn't mind living alone but felt that something was missing. I wanted to share my life with someone special. So in the second half of my life I decided to start dating again.

I didn't think it would be too hard to discover a companion who would suit me. I had just started a new career — as a resident doctor in Boston training as a psychiatrist. I was 95 pounds of energy. My credentials were great. I was living in a city of smart people. Find a boyfriend? Piece of cake!

Boy, was I wrong! I began by placing an ad in the monthly city magazine. My ad read exactly as I saw myself: "Physician, artist, writer. Smart, slim, sane. Likes to listen, cook, and rollerblade. Are you the right man? 45–55." Responses poured in by phone and through the mail. I weeded out those who seemed mentally ill, were unemployed, or peppered our chat with digs at their last wife. I was determined to give everyone else a chance.

My first months in the dating scene were tedious and disappointing. I had dinner with men who spent the entire meal talking about themselves, or worse, their evil ex-wives, their troubled kids, and their tyrannical bosses. One fellow graphically detailed his prostate troubles (after all, I was a doctor and should understand). Another date had a criminal record, another was disbarred. The man with the Yale law degree started yelling at me for no reason.

By the time I moved to Seattle four years later, I was still looking. I placed ads in a monthly magazine, the weekly newspaper, and the *Jewish News*. After training as a psychiatrist, my screening process had improved. I learned it was best to try to get to know a little bit about the man before we met. If I could easily slip it into the phone conversation, I would ask him about his last relationship. I added this question to my list after a date with a man whose wife had died three weeks before. I listened for phrases like "between jobs" and "anger management;" these were warnings to go no further.

I also learned that being older had its

drawbacks. Even though I'm downright skinny, men were disappointed by the fact that my skin was not wrinkle-free. I didn't even bother to meet the man who wanted to start a second family.

But I kept at it, perfecting my techniques. Jay was response number 751. Really! We met when he answered my personal ad. He had to accommodate my lack of interest in basketball and I had to get used to his Nordic silences but five years later I still appreciate my artist boyfriend.

Success at last

I learned a lot in my quest for a relationship as an "older woman." And that's why I wrote this book. To share this information with other mature men and women, many of whom have given up on the prospect of romance.

When I look around at my patients and friends over 50, I see energetic people with a lot to offer the world. They have jobs, careers, varied interests. Many view their lives as rich and full. The only thing missing is a loving relationship.

For some, even the thought of dating at 50 seems ludicrous. Others have tried it but experienced many disappointments.

11

I, too, have experienced those awful moments of discouragement. While I was actively dating, I was sometimes rejected out of hand, because I was "too old." It's depressing when potential partners your age say they're looking for someone younger. Suddenly the world seems full of people who are more youthful, thin and self-assured.

How can you learn to feel hopeful and dignified — and find love?

To answer this question, I developed a three-pronged solution: knowledge, action and attitude. Once I had the formula, I tried it out and fine tuned the technique. Over the years, I never gave up. Using my skills as a psychiatrist and relying on the support of my friends, I collected the required information, took the necessary steps, and kept an open mind. And I succeeded. I found a satisfying and lasting relationship. Then I began helping others do the same.

Now, I'm delighted to share my findings with you. This book will help you resist loneliness and empower you to discover romance, whether or not you choose to find another spouse, or are content to live alone. Be hopeful. There is love, companionship, and satisfaction at the end of your quest. Be brave, and follow the Bible's advice: "Choose life, so that you may live."

⤝ 1 ⤞

A Change of Attitude

Great! You've decided you don't want to be alone. You've considered getting a dog, but a golden retriever can do only so much. Sharing life with a human is what you have in mind. You miss the comfort of companionship, someone who asks about your day. You want to celebrate your successes over dinner; you want to be needed and comforted in tough times. You yearn to feel appreciated and special, to know your opinion counts, to feel the warmth of someone's arm around your shoulder. Loving is an important component of daily life, and there is no age limit on wanting it.

An optimistic attitude is one of the most important factors in successful dating. In this chapter, I dispel the common myths that keep older people from even trying.

Myth #1: "All the good ones are taken."

This is the most common excuse I hear from people over 50 who are not dating. Although it's true the population of available singles narrows with age, there are still many potential partners out there.

Statistics are on your side

There are 21 million single men and women over 50 in the US today. And as our life expectancies lengthen, the percentage of the population over 50 goes up and up. The number of older Americans has more than tripled in the past century. By 2030, one out of every five people will be over the age of 65.

The average life expectancy is 73 years for men and 80 years for women. Keep in mind, this is an average; many men and women will live beyond these ages. In fact, the "oldest, old" (people classified by sociologists as over 85) is 25 times larger than it was in 1900 and is growing faster than any other age group.

If you're a woman, you may be wondering about the disparity in gender. It's true that men, on average, have a shorter life expectancy than women so there are twice as many single women as single men between the ages of 50 and 74.

However, when you consider the absolute numbers, the picture brightens. We're not looking at one small cocktail party where you scan the room and see a dozen hungry women to every man. In reality there are 14 million single women and seven million unattached men, so it would be more like a cocktail party with the guests in the ratio of two women for every man.

But not every woman is looking for companionship. Many are content to remain single. If you look at the Internet as a dating resource, you find men over 50 searching for company far outnumber women seekers.

Also, the population of mature singles is dynamic. You might think you've looked in all the right places and found no one, but new people arrive on the scene all the time. Spouses die. Marriages and relationships fall apart. People move into town. Retirement suddenly opens up new possibilities for those who previously focused their energy on work. Too busy with family, career, and friends, unattached singles may not be looking today. But they may be ready tomorrow.

When 62-year-old Charles retired as high school principal, he kept busy working as an educational consultant, hiking on the weekends and spending a lot of time with his nieces and nephews. But he had always wanted to get married and now he felt time was running out. Outside of a few short romances, he had lived alone most of his life and had little experience with women.

His sister and his best friend convinced him to start actively looking for a partner. They helped him write personal ads that he placed in the local newspaper and on an Internet dating site. Many women he met were suspicious about why he had never married. He found this ironic. "What? You think I would be a better match if I had gone through a miserable divorce? Think of me instead as an unspoiled commodity!"

Be patient. At first, some people appear undesirable or unavailable. People who are dealing with illness, grieving a loss, or having problems at work need time to heal. But with time you may find in one of these people a new friend or a romance.

That said, in my opinion, those already in committed relationships are off limits. If a man or woman has troubles with a current partner and solves them by getting involved with you, the pattern is likely to repeat itself. Focus your efforts instead on those who are actually available.

Don't be a victim of your own fears — of the mistaken notion that the odds are against your finding a companion. Your frustrations may be real, but your chances for success are excellent.

Myth #2: "No one will love me the way I am."

It's natural to have misgivings. You say to yourself, "How can someone love me the way I am now? How can I make it work if I never have before?" Thoughts like these — and worse — cross the mind of even the most confident person.

The difficulty of finding a relationship in youth is compounded by the complexities of aging. By midlife, losses can accumulate. Careers flounder, stress mounts, marriages end, good health fades. If intimacy was elusive in youth, it's no easier to find with age. Isolation increases. Energy wanes. Retirement can mean less money and more empty time to fill.

But consider this: wouldn't it be easier

to deal with these problems with the help of a loving companion? The most vulnerable people in old age are those who have not resolved these internal and interpersonal conflicts.

Self-acceptance instead of self-help

You don't have to become more spiritual, more social, or more confident to find a partner. Don't squander your energy trying to become a new person. Seeking a makeover implies you are unacceptable. Assume that you're more than good enough.

Age has its advantages. By now you know your interests and limitations. Your self-awareness, gained through years of experience, is a great ally in your search. If you decide to make any changes during your quest, it is because you choose to do what is practical.

Certain behaviors may stand in the way of finding a special someone. You can learn to identify your problem areas and gently make changes. If you're famous for your short temper, you might identify the things that set you off and avoid them. If you have bad breath, visit your dentist and ask what you can do to alleviate the problem. If you dress in shabby or unflattering clothes, increase your options by sprucing up your appearance.

Overweight? Losing thirty pounds before placing a personal ad is less practical. Start an exercise program (you might meet someone at your aerobics class or at the gym), buy some flattering clothes and look for that special person who cares more about your personality than your waistline.

It's more productive to work at looking better rather than thinner. For women who want encouragement to accept themselves the way they are, I recommend Katie Arons' bestselling book, *Being Sexy at Any Size*.

Perhaps you want to change certain personality traits. It's not too late. If you're timid, taking a course from Toastmasters or Dale Carnegie may help you become more self-assured and widen your social circle at the same time.

It's possible to alter even the most troublesome idiosyncrasies. Although there's no guarantee, major changes can happen through effort and commitment to long-term psychotherapy or psychoanalysis.

Ben had a difficult childhood with a critical mother who told him constantly that he was worthless. As an adult, he found himself treating others the same way. He alienated friends and girlfriends with his crabby outlook and nasty verbal digs.

Ben knows he has to change this attitude or he will drive away prospective partners. He's in therapy but he's also dating, trying out new behaviors. He takes it one date at a time, keeping his judgments to himself and hoping to make it to a second date.

Maury admits his problem with jealousy. After years of psychotherapy he understands where it came from. His mother favored his younger brother, who she thought was smarter and better looking than Maury. Despite a good job in engineering and an active social life, Maury has never gotten over this early insult. He says, "I feel something like an electric shock go through me when I watch my girlfriend talk to another man." It doesn't help that he's always been attracted to beautiful, younger women. His current girlfriend, Monica is 40 to his 58.

But Maury was honest about his jealousy when he started dating Monica. She understands why he questions her after she has an animated conversation with the clerk in the grocery store. She assures Maury that he's her guy and she doesn't intend to flirt. As their relationship develops, Maury is becoming more trusting and Monica feels less need to be defensive.

Myth #3: "My family won't understand."

When you're ready to begin dating, those close to you may be ambivalent or downright discouraging. They want to see you happy but they may feel your dating is disloyal to a departed or deceased spouse. Children, especially, may need time to adapt to a parent's new single status.

While you want to respect the feelings of your children and grandchildren, also consider how a new relationship might benefit everyone. If you've withdrawn or become needier after your loss, the support of a new relationship may make you more accessible to your family. Sharing responsibilities with another will reduce your stress. And it's good for everyone to see you proclaim your right to personal happiness.

Pauline had been widowed for five years. Her husband Arthur died only a few months after being diagnosed with a brain tumor, leaving Pauline as a single parent of two unruly and angry teenage boys. To make matters worse, Arthur hadn't left behind much money and Pauline was struggling to make ends meet while keeping her boys out of trouble. Scott, her eldest son, spent most of his time away from home while her younger boy, Steven, kept getting picked up by the police for shoplifting, trespassing and other minor crimes.

Barry knew Pauline from working with her in a church volunteer group and offered to help make some badly needed repairs on her home as a way of getting to

> *"Age has its advantages. By now you know your interests and limitations. Your self-awareness, gained through years of experience, is a great ally in your search."*

know her. Pauline wasn't interested in dating, at first, but she found herself appreciating the company and support of another adult. As she grew fonder of Barry, her sons treated him worse. Scott, now 20, would get up and leave, always with some transparent excuse, when Barry arrived, while 16-year-old Steven was critical and rude to his mother's boyfriend.

Barry had his own family problems. After a bitter divorce, his wife had discouraged him from seeing his only daughter who, even after she turned 18, refused to see her father.

It seemed like Barry and Pauline would have to be content with occasional nights out since her sons made it so unpleasant for Barry to spend time with her at home. Then Scott was in a serious motorcycle accident. Barry was the only person who could comfort Steven, who was afraid he was going to lose his brother like he had his father.

As Scott recovered his health, the three men started spending time together. Barry was around to help Scott with his rehab exercises and to drive Steven back and forth to school. As Barry slowly found a place for himself in the family, Pauline's sons began to realize their mother's relationship with Barry had improved their lives. And Barry got a second chance at parenting.

Myth #4: "My sex life is over."

Sex improves with age. Many older adults report that sex is as good as or even better than it was when they were 40. The frequency of climax for women increases with each decade into their 80s. Even though men have less forceful ejaculations, and need more time for a repeat erection, they still enjoy orgasm. A slower pace allows both partners to savor the pleasure longer.

Age also provides more free time, fewer children, and no concerns about pregnancy. However mature adults still have to worry about sexually transmitted diseases. These risks do not diminish with age.

Whereas frequency of activity may decline with age, specialists in sex and aging say 70% of people over 60 who have regular partners have sex at least once a month. A survey, conducted by the AARP in 1999, found that one out of four people over 75 engage in weekly sexual intercourse.

Sex is good for you. Men who experience frequent orgasm have a 50% lower risk of death. Active sex burns up to 300 calories, works muscles, boosts the body's immune system and just plain feels good. Sex aids in pain relief by releasing helpful body chemicals such as endorphins and cortisone. Women over 60 who have frequent sex — through intercourse or masturbation — have fewer problems with vaginal dryness. Older men who have regular sex achieve faster erections. The American Heart Association finds no contraindications to sex.

Viagra, introduced in 1998, and similar prescription medications have boosted men's performance. Hormone replacement therapies and supplementary lubricants ease the physical discomfort which sometimes accompanies menopause. If you're experiencing any difficulties, talk to your doctor. Age does not have to mean a decline in libido or sexual activity.

Just because sex is an option, doesn't mean you have to indulge. You may simply crave the warmth and closeness that can be found in a relationship. It's okay if all you want to do is cuddle or hold hands. Read Chapter 8 for details!

Myth #5: "Dating is dangerous."

You have the power to avoid harm. With thought and practice, you can recognize hazardous situations and take control. You don't need a black belt to keep from getting hurt.

Your first date is often a meeting with someone you know only through contact by e-mail and telephone. This man or woman certainly won't be carrying a note from a psychiatrist certifying the bearer to be sane and safe. Ask questions on the telephone before you meet. This can be awkward, but it's more comfortable to make this assessment from a distance, rather than in person. And, for the first meeting, always meet your dates in a public place.

In Chapters 3, 4 and 5, you'll learn exactly what to ask and how to phrase your questions.

You will become skilled at reading signals and find out how to respond to them. You'll learn how to ask for help, if you have problems, and how to extract yourself from a situation before it gets unmanageable.

There is also the issue of emotional safety. Some men — as well as some women — prey on the vulnerable. They target singles' events, looking to score sexual success or financial gain. People newly single or chronically lonely are game for people with bad intentions. Read Chapter 6 to learn to recognize signs of danger and how to avoid trouble.

Myth #6: "Dating leads to marriage."

It's okay to want to stay single. You don't have to be looking for love. Maybe you had a 25-year marriage and now only want a date for social events. Maybe you think of true love as something you shared with a certain someone and now you'd be happy with an intermittent companion. Wanting less shouldn't keep you from seeking company. It's fair to everyone, though, to be honest about your intentions.

Redefining dating

Many people who have not looked for a partner for years are put off by the thought of "dating." In the 1950s, dating was simply the first step in a progression that led to engagement and then marriage. By the 1970s, a date was just as likely to end with casual sex without any implied promise to meet again. But now, dating covers a wide range of possibilities and choices, from the most casual coffee hour to a shared trip to Hawaii. Rather than conforming to some popular notions of what a date should be, define it to suit yourself.

For whatever reason — and remember you don't need to justify your needs or feelings — you may want to date but don't feel ready for any attachments. Meet new people for coffee and nothing more. If you want to maintain these contacts but keep your distance, stay in touch through occasional phone calls or e-mail and casual meetings when convenient.

Dating can also mean sharing activities and even sex with a number of companions. Your goal may be to get to know an assortment of people without committing to anyone. Some use the word dating to mean "going steady," but not living, with one companion. Perhaps you share an evening or two a week. You may spend holidays and vacations together but return to your own homes afterwards. Some men and women have had a successful long-term relationship but don't want to duplicate it. Others prefer living alone.

Sam was one of these. He had lived with women all his life: first his mother and his sisters, then with the wife whom he married right after high school. That marriage didn't last and neither did the two after it. After three lost houses and two alimonies, Sam decided to give up on marriage. He didn't want to risk losing his home again or the pain of living in an atmosphere fraught with conflict.

But Sam wasn't ready to give up on romance. He's been dating Lucia for over a year. From the start, he made it clear to her that they would never move in together. Sometimes she hints that it would be cheaper if they shared expenses. "This is the best I can do," he tells her. "We have good times, sex is fine, there isn't anyone else, my family love you and so do I. But this will only work for me if we live in separate places."

Sam is clear about his needs, although perhaps that will change with time. For many people, this sort of arrangement will shift and your date will become your "old man" or "old lady," the charming, old-fashioned term for a person who shares living space without the legal bind of marriage. You may find yourself staying over more nights a week than not. First you're given a spot on the night table for your book, then a drawer for spare underwear, and finally, your own closet. And, voila! You're living together and it's totally painless.

Contrary to popular belief, today's older men are more likely to seek a permanent liaison, while women, after losing a relationship, are more inclined to declare, and then preserve, their independent status. Many women have spent a lifetime cultivating friendships. These connections serve them well when a man is out of the picture. They remain in the workforce longer and are more assertive. Older men, on the other hand, are in far more of a hurry to replace their missing partner.

As you begin your search, don't look too far into the future. Your best strategy is to figure out where you stand right now. What kind of relationship would suit you best today? If you aren't sure, make a checklist of questions. Itemize your needs. Put this list in a drawer and revisit it from time to time.

Keep in mind you don't have to give in to cultural pressure or the expectations of family and friends. Be realistic about how much closeness you can tolerate. Everyone has a different capacity for intimacy at various stages of life. Remember you have no obligation to conform to any imaginary ideal of commitment.

Will and Joyce are both 60. Joyce had one bad marriage. Will avoided commitments, after watching his friends go through painful divorces. It took a while but this couple finally found an arrangement that works for them. They rent apartments around the corner from each other and spend most weekends and vacations together. "This is about as much closeness as we can stand," says Will. They rely on each other in stressful times. Joyce was there for him when he had heart surgery, and he was with her when her brother died.

They also both date, and sometimes are intimate, with other people. "We're getting older and we don't want to miss out on any friendships before life is over," explains Will. Although this arrangement might not work for everyone, it works for them.

There's always room for change. One kind of relationship can easily shift to another. It's your choice. As long as you avoid hurtful behavior and admit your intentions, you can enjoy your own style of dating free of excuses and guilt.

✦ 2 ✦

Taking the First Steps

To succeed in dating after the age of 50, all you have to do is figure out what appeals to you and take the first steps. With 19 million other unattached people over 50, you can draw from the large pool of singles available through advertising, dating services, social clubs, and singles' activities. You should also spread the word through your network of family and friends: let them know you're looking.

New attitudes toward midlife romance emerge as the population ages. It's increasingly acceptable for older people to admit to seeking romance and enjoying sex. We are far from the end of the line just because we're past 50. Loneliness doesn't have to be the companion of age.

At times in your search, you may feel desperate. Just remember almost everyone has endured a bad date and suffered from rejection. With luck, your feelings are temporary and will pass.

Are you ready?

Mature singles are preoccupied with their jobs, families, health and other important activities. But if having a companion is your goal, don't postpone the search. Begin as soon as you are ready. It takes time to polish rusty skills and learn new ones.

Maybe you are putting off dating until you lose weight. Or begin exercising. Or stop feeling bad about your last relationship. These are all valid reasons, but they won't get you any closer to your goal. If you want to begin dating, you should take a deep breath and start. It's just like dancing. If you want to dance, you can't stand around watching. You have to pick a partner, gather your courage and ask.

You might need more time if you've just lost a significant relationship. Everyone feels hurt, anger, and disappointment after a breakup. If you're feeling betrayed, you may find it hard to trust again. It's important to acknowledge your feelings. But don't stay stuck in sorrow or anger about the past.

Forgiving those who harmed you may help you move forward. Research shows that forgiving wrongs, an act easier for

33

women than men, has health benefits, perhaps because relinquishing grudges reduces stress. This doesn't mean you can't be angry. It does mean you can set the past aside and be open to new people treating you with kindness and respect.

Self-forgiveness is important too. If you treated someone poorly in the past or feel the breakup was caused by your actions, you may be reluctant to try again for fear of doing future damage. However, no two relationships are the same. Your next partner will be different, and so will you — changed by your experiences.

Elena had had a miserable marriage. She was a loving, old-fashioned woman who spent a great deal of energy trying to turn her icy, self-absorbed husband into a warmer, kinder man. After 33 years of marriage, she finally got the courage to tell him she wanted a divorce. At first, she found going to the grocery store alone bewildering. It took almost a year before she was prepared to date.

Now at 63, she is beginning to enjoy her independence. She goes to singles' parties and out on coffee dates. Salsa lessons have taken priority over crochet. Weeks in advance, she's letting her dance partners know that she's available for New Year's

Eve. But she's not ready to marry again, and she's not sure she'll ever be. "I prefer playing the field," she says. "I don't want to commit to one man." Last month, one of her dates accused her of "leading him on." Since then, she tells each new man she meets about her preferences. If he doesn't accept her need for independence, she crosses him off her list.

Grieving a loss

If you're recently widowed or your long-term companion has just left, you need time to mourn. Don't think about losing yourself in a new relationship, hoping you can forget your grief. It's unfair to everyone if you're comparing your new prospect with the person you lost.

Some men and women suppose wanting new love is disloyal to the absent partner. Some believe love happens only once in a lifetime. If you've lost a spouse through death, ask yourself whether your past partner would want you to be lonely. What if you had died? Would you want your mate to remain alone? Keep in mind you are not trying to replace the old love. A new and unique connection doesn't invalidate the past. It brings delight in its own right.

After a bereavement, you may crave solitude. But the need to be alone gradually shifts to an increasing desire to be with others. As soon as you recognize this shift, go ahead and socialize. Note: socialize does not mean "fall in love" or "make love." Look for others who are at the same stage in the grieving process. Attend a support group for the newly widowed or divorced. You may

> *"If you're recently widowed or your long-term companion has just left, you need time to mourn. Don't think about losing yourself in a new relationship, hoping you can forget your grief."*

find such programs offered by your local church or synagogue. Volunteer.

You don't have to bear your pain alone, yet dating shouldn't be your chief goal. Seek people, like yourself, who have passed through the phase of acute grief but aren't ready for new attachments. Your connections may only last as long as you share mutual concerns, or evolve into something deeper. Keep expectations low. Your goal is to feel less alone. You can find pleasure in companionship even while feeling pain. Remember: friendship first, love later. You'll know when the time is right.

Do postpone placing or answering an ad soon after a recent trauma, such as divorce, separation, death or the onset of an illness. It's tempting to use ads as a fantasy-fix for life's miseries. But there is no way to by-pass the natural process of mourning. It is inconsiderate toward your future dates, since you're not ready to give full attention to a new relationship. Even if you are con-vinced you are ready, the other person may have difficulty believing you.

When I was living in Boston, a 65-year-old surgeon answered my personal ad and invited me to go to the flower show on a first date. Even though he was much older than I preferred, I accepted since I knew his profession and the hospital where he worked. He picked me up and as we were driving to the show, he reached across the seat and took my hand. It was completely inappropriate as we had just met a half hour earlier. While we were strolling down the aisles at the flower show, he tried to put his arm around my shoulder. I de-clared my interest in carnivorous plants, hoping I could get some breathing space, but he insisted on going with me to find them. Finally I asked him to take me home. On the way there, he told me his wife had died only two weeks before. This was the date that convinced me to ask about previous relationships, whenever possible, before meeting someone.

Know the signs that indicate you're ready for a new relationship. You need time to review events, mull over mistakes and stop feeling angry or sad. Consider your answers to the following questions: Am I seeking a replacement that looks and acts like my deceased partner because I want to recreate the past? Am I looking for a replacement that looks and acts exactly opposite to my last partner in an effort to avoid making the same mistakes because, if I find such a person I can repair my lost connection? Am I ready to stop talking about my last relationship? Do I have the ability to enjoy life alone? Has anyone I trusted said, "Isn't it time you find another companion?" It's a good sign when an outsider senses you're ready.

The benefits of experience

Remember the first house you bought? The view from the living room window was so great, it hardly mattered that the furnace was rickety and the attic housed mice. You fell for the pretty façade. After buying and selling over the years, your goals changed. You listened to the inspector who said the roof would never last. You gave up exquisite kitchen cabinets in favor of reliable plumbing. Now you live in a comfortable place.

Except for "resale value," choosing your second house has much in common with selecting your second companion. You now have the benefit of experience. You know passionate love, although marvelous, cannot be sustained with the original intensity. You recognize that comfortable love endures and deepens with time. Friendship, support and shared interests win over the need for perpetual stimulation. You'd rather feel secure than ride the roller-coaster of infatuation and disappointment that characterized your first love affairs.

You are surer of your identity than you were in your youth. You know yourself well, if not perfectly. You recognize what you can tolerate and what drives you bonkers. You're clear about what is not negotiable but willing to compromise on the rest. Glamour and romance have become less satisfying than the pleasure of compatibility. Your hard-won wisdom simplifies the process of dating.

Knowing your limitations and expectations makes it easier to find the right person. Think about what you like and what is unacceptable. Can you be in the company of a man who doesn't talk? Can you stand a woman who's flirtatious? Maybe you're not sure if qualities you found troublesome in the past still bother you. Experiment. Going out on a half dozen dates is not the same as promising to walk down the aisle.

Know yourself

By the time you've reached 50, you may have noticed that you have certain patterns in relationships. Often our choices are influenced by our childhood. Romantic involvements are mini-stages on which we act out battles for attention, expressions of anger, and yearnings for love from half a century ago.

Edward grew up with a nagging, demanding mother. Nothing he ever did pleased her. When he was young, she criticized about his performance in school. When he was in college, he didn't call enough. She even complained about the presents he gave her at Christmas — they were always the wrong size or the wrong color.

Edward had a series of relationships with women who were as critical and demanding as his mother. Or he fell for women who were completely unavailable, like the stunning 25 year-old administrative assistant in his office or the married woman lawyer who worked down the hall.

Like many of us, Edward selected a potential partner with his primary caretaker's qualities. This happens not because we want to be plagued by our childhood tormentors but because we are trying to create a reparative experience. We mistakenly believe we have the power to alter the past. We think we can get it right the second time around and get the love and admiration we craved.

Unfortunately this strategy never works. Edward chose women so much like his mother that no matter how well he behaved they would find fault with him. Or he fell for women who were completely inaccessible, thus preventing him from engaging in the battle to please.

Edward was unwilling to look at these patterns in therapy but he did find a compromise. Edward had bad luck in love but was a champ at making friends — he had many male and female friends who demanded much less attention than a girlfriend might. Ramona, a retired school teacher, was one of them. Although Ramona, who had her own difficult personal history to overcome, knew Edward was not a good match, she enjoyed going to concerts with him and they relied on each other during difficult times. Sometimes she even spent the night. Each played the best game with the cards they were dealt.

Change is possible for people past fifty. But like joint flexibility, personal pliability diminishes as the years pass. Although individual growth occurs when we partner in our twenties, that's less true as we age. By the time we're 50, it's more realistic to evaluate a relationship based on how well our lives blend, rather than expecting change.

Pursuing a dream

Do passion, drama, and charisma feature prominently in your search? Just because you're older doesn't mean you've given up longing for that dream partner. Do you still require that slim woman with long hair? Do you want to run your fingers through his curls? Your dream can still come true, if you're willing to adjust the hair color of your ideal partner to gray.

Older lovers hold up a different mirror to each other. These lines from John Donne's 17th century elegy are still applicable today:

> *Neither spring nor summer beauty hath*
> *such grace*
> *As I have seen in one autumnal face.*

If you didn't come across your fantasy partner at 20, success is even more remote a half-century later. Your best chance at finding a relationship is to aspire to what is reasonable for you for today.

Sometimes having high standards for physical beauty can lead to emotional and financial distress. Paul is a successful physician who looks 55 but is really ten years older. After many unsuccessful attempts to find an American wife, he began pursuing Russian women through an agency that makes such matches. His quest is expensive — he must pay the agency fee and his airfare to Russia to meet prospective brides as well as buy gifts for their families. His first match was Tanya, a stunning blonde. When they met in Moscow, he was put off by the massive quantities of alcohol she consumed. His second match, Natalya, looked down her nose at the expensive watches he brought as gifts for her family. Expensive jewelry wasn't enough. She expected him to pay for the relocation of her parents and her five siblings. He invited the third woman, Maria, to live with him in Los Angeles. "What a disaster!" he declares. "She turned out to be hysterical and nasty. She spent almost all of her time at the shopping mall." He sent her home but still mourns over his loss. "She had such a great figure." Paul may be doomed to failure if he keeps on placing such a high priority on appearances.

As a rule, fantasies don't age well. But every rule has exceptions. Even though the odds are against you, you might still want to pursue your dream. Can you modify your wishes but still remain within dream range? Can you change the venue in which you search? If you're flexible, nothing is impossible.

Explore new possibilities

Think of your new dating project as an opportunity. If success has eluded you in the past, this is a good time to figure out why. Look at the circumstances of previous relationships, notice what precipitated breakups and ask if it's possible to do things differently. Examine the attachments that went wrong in the past. Were they truly connections that met your needs? Or were you conforming to social pressure or trying to live up to the expectations of others? Reevaluate your goals and the methods you tried to use to reach them. What worked and what failed?

Anne-Marie, an elegant, savvy, and self-sufficient woman, who runs her own consulting business, spent her life pursuing "smart" men, because she wanted someone who could match her level of intellectual achievement (she has a Ph.D. in Political Science). She had two long-term relationships and one marriage with professional men: a dentist, a surgeon, and a top trial lawyer. But each of these relationships was difficult — her partners were complicated, demanding, even competitive — and ultimately failed.

When Anne-Marie turned 58, she decided it might be wiser to choose a man for his heart rather than his brain. Her new lover, Billy, is a house painter. He spends his spare time reading history and winning bridge tournaments. He's easygoing, likes to laugh, and is a good listener. "Far more important," says Anne-Marie, "he genuinely likes me."

Because of the disparity between them, in income and age (he's nine years younger), her friends warned he was "using" her. But their relationship has lasted for over two years. They spend a lot of time together but maintain separate places. "We're not ready to live together yet," Anne-Marie says. "Neither of us is in a rush. Yet it feels like a real partnership. I may be contributing more money, but I'm getting so much in return that it feels equal."

Your requirements may have been fairly rigid up until now. You would date only men who earned above a certain income or women not a pound over a particular weight. Again, let me remind you how vital it is to be flexible. In the long run, you have little to lose. You can always forget your experiment and return to your previous standards.

Martin was reluctant to accompany his friend to a singles' dance. He thought the women who attended such events would all be brittle blondes, wearing flashy clothes and too much makeup. And at first, Virginia, who bleaches her hair and wears bright red lipstick, fit his stereotype. But when they started dancing, he appreciated her honesty. Virginia didn't tell him how fun he was (he wasn't) or what a great dancer he was (he wasn't). Instead, she confessed she prefers square dancing, which happens to be Martin's favorite too. They've since become partners in dancing, as well as in life.

The school of dating

Being older and wiser doesn't necessarily make you an expert on love. Maybe you had one, happy multi-decade marriage that ended because your spouse died. Or maybe your history is made up of a succession of brief romances. No matter what kind of relationships you've had, no matter how much experience you've gained, you still have things to learn.

Treat your quest like taking a class in a new subject. Imagine you've enrolled in a political science course. Of course you're not a novice at current events. You've followed the news all your life. But you've signed up for this class to deepen your

47

knowledge, to put events in historical perspective and to meet others with similar interests.

Don't assume everyone else knows more than you. If they were already experts, you would be reading their columns in *The Nation* or the *New York Times*. Instead, they are sitting next to you and asking to borrow your notes.

Consider yourself a beginner in the class of daters. You and your classmates will make mistakes. A blunder doesn't mean you've failed for life. You can correct your mistakes, if not with the current date, with the next.

As part of your education, remember what didn't work in the past. For example, you can predict disaster if you connect with women who put their families first and you last on the list. Or you know you cannot be involved with a man who will see you only one night a weekend, leaving you yearning for company the rest of the week. If you disliked the way your previous partner always deferred to you in making choices about activities, food, or sex with the phrase "It's up to you" — the older generation's equivalent of "whatever" — select a man who is willing to make his preferences known.

Develop a plan

If you were looking for employment, you would approach this task using a well-organized and methodical process. You would draft a resume, read ads, interview, and prepare to reject the unacceptable. You'd check in with friends who would listen to your adventures and be sympathetic during rough times. You'd take some risks and avoid others. You might find what seems to be the perfect job, and later decide it doesn't suit you. Or you might get turned down for your dream job.

Treat dating the same way. And remember: signing up for either a job or a date isn't irrevocable. Even though it's easier said than done, don't take rejection as a personal affront. As in the employment arena, you cannot possibly control the preferences and quirks of others. You know in advance some of your efforts will succeed and others will fail. But if you don't succeed at first, you can try again.

Eric was a retired corporate executive. An athlete in college, he had always dated women who shared his interests in skiing and kayaking. After his second double by-pass operation, he decided he had to slow down, so he looked for women with different interests. He went out with Elsie for a month. They both liked to read and cook, but he was bored. Then he dated Kathy, an active aerobics instructor, but found her stamina dangerously exceeded his. So he tried again with a woman who would rather be at the opera than in a kayak. "For whatever magical reason, Sara and I clicked," Eric says. "I'm glad I tried again."

Enjoy the process

If you want a relationship, make your search the priority. Strategize with lists of places to go, people to contact and methods for meeting available singles. Don't be ashamed of coveting a companion. It's okay to focus on your personal life.

Your mission should never become so intensive you don't have a chance to evaluate each new prospect thoughtfully. If you were looking for a job, you would become dizzy if you had an interview every twenty minutes.

It's bewildering if you meet too many men or women in a short period. Many dates can seem like good choices. Slow down and focus on a few possibilities.

You stand a better chance of success if you eliminate the "comparison shopping" element from the dating experience. Romance doesn't blossom when you (or your date) feel like you are being tried on and possibly discarded, like one more coat on a rack.

Rodney was methodical in his search. He put a personal ad in his local weekly paper and got responses from 75 women interested in a 65-year-old man who likes fine dining and walks by the sea (even though Iowa is about as far from the ocean as you can get). Overwhelmed by the possibilities, Rodney made a list of the women he wanted to date and gave them a priority ranking, based on their physical descriptions, occupations, and common interests. He also kept track of who he called, what they said, and how he felt after the conversation. After each date, he rushed to his desk to make notes about what happened. Then he ranked the women again on the basis of the dates. Unfortunately after dating thirty women, he couldn't keep them straight. They were a blur in his mind.

One of Rodney's top priorities was finding a professional woman under the age of 45. His next door neighbor, Marla, a waitress, would never have made his list on both counts. But every time they met in the laundry room, she asked him about his search. She listened to his trials and tribulations, encouraged him to keep going, and sympathized with his desire for companionship. One evening, they got so involved in conversation that he invited her upstairs to his apartment to continue their talk. That's when he realized Marla had moved to the top of his list.

Searching in all the right places

People over 50 have many ways to meet a companion or lover. Ask the person sitting next to you in the doctor's office about their preference in vitamins. Cruise the salad bar in a grocery store — it's a whole lot easier than trolling a singles' bar. You can pass the person more than once, chat about veggies, and then exchange phone numbers at the checkout.

Years ago, churches were the only place a single senior could be on the lookout for love. Today, you can belong to a growing number of active adult retirement communities and clubs. For example, one over-55 community in Palm Desert, CA, boasts 53 social groups. Join a sports club or get involved in an activity such as birding, bridge, art, drama, cooking, or political discussion groups. Volunteer. You can also take or give classes.

Be ready to expand your repertoire. Try something new. Register for workshops on communication or relationships. Find seminars devoted to dating after 50 at community centers and community colleges where you learn new skills and, as a bonus, meet others with a similar goal.

Not every activity is suitable for an older

> *"Consider yourself a beginner in the class of daters. You and your classmates will make mistakes. A blunder doesn't mean you've failed for life. You can correct your mistakes, if not with the current date, with the next."*

crowd. Health clubs are a fine place for young folks, but most men and women past 50 feel their bodies won't withstand scrutiny in Spandex. Grown-ups find their own haunts. Dance studios and clubs are a ready source of partners. No experience is required when lessons are offered. Usually dancers are encouraged to change partners so you can dance with every one in the room.

Speed-dating is a concept that originated in LA as a meeting method for Jewish singles and is now a popular nondenominational activity. Men and women are paired up for six-minute chats, then move on to another person when a bell rings. In a short time, you meet many new people. At the end of the event, you have a chance to reconnect with those you'd like to know better. Older singles can also meet online and in printed personals. Afraid of placing or answering ads? Chapters 3 and 4 will help you make use of these excellent sources of social life.

Remember, one exposure isn't enough. You need to attend the same activity more than once. Return visits add to your comfort and permit others to recognize you as a familiar and friendly face. Plan to return at least three times before you scrap any activity as a waste of time.

Know that failures are unavoidable. Prepare yourself to withstand the inevitable. Think about how you will handle disappointment. Will you discuss your feelings with friends? Do you have a plan to move on to the next date or singles' activity?

Laura, a 55-year-old school secretary, was not having much luck on the dating scene. Every time she met a man for a date, he told her she was "not his type." She knew they were referring to her age and her weight. Then she met Kofi. He was standing behind her in the grocery checkout line, with almost the same items in his basket as she had in hers. They started talking about their mutual love of baking and decided to get together to share recipes.

Even though they come from very different backgrounds — Kofi is from Nigeria, Laura from New England — they enjoy many of the same things, especially cooking. A favorite date for them is spending the day in the kitchen, working on a complicated recipe.

Kofi doesn't care that Laura is older than he is (by 15 years) or that she is overweight. "In his culture, heavier women are prized, not rejected," Laura says. "I never thought I'd find love with someone so different."

You, too, can find the kind of relationship you seek — whether it's a coffee date or a life partner. There are no guarantees and no hard-and-fast rules to insure success. You'll have to struggle at times to keep up your spirits. You'll have to forge ahead in uncharted territory. Remember: you are not alone in your search for love.

❦ 3 ❧

Yes! You Should Advertise

In her fifties, Evelyn survived an unpleasant divorce, adjusted to early retirement from the school district, and recovered from hip replacement surgery. Despite the fact her joints were aging, her heart was still young. She was tired of being the odd person at dinner parties and her friends were tired of hearing her complain about how she never met any decent men.

One day one of her girlfriends handed her a newspaper with a personal ad circled in red. "Don't call me until you call him," she said. Evelyn liked Jerry's ad. He wasn't looking for a good-looking blonde babe twenty years his junior. He wanted a woman who would like his garden and his cat and who shared his interest in film. Evelyn knew on their first movie date that she had finally found a keeper.

Although many older people feel uncomfortable about the idea of meeting someone through advertising, an option not available to us in our younger days, it has many advantages. While the search process can be awkward, sheer volume and anonymity help ease the sting of rejection and increase your chances of success. Whether seeking a lifetime partner, a casual dinner date, a pen pal, or e-pal, many people of all ages find success meeting others through personal ads.

The odds are in your favor

In the over-55-age range, according to the 2000 U.S. Census, there are seven million separated, divorced, widowed, or never married men compared to 14 million unattached women. It's natural to conclude older men, who often advertise for younger women, have a much better chance of finding a new relationship than a single woman.

But numbers don't tell the whole story. For one thing, statisticians can't tell how many of those singles want to stay single and how many are seeking relationships. Unattached men are more likely to seek a new partner than solo women who often enjoy their independence and the company of their friends.

The numbers for personal ads are much more encouraging. More and more single men and women in the over-50 age group are placing personal ads, and the gender balance is surprising. As of January, 2001, America OnLine boasted 46,000 ads in the over-50 category, from an equal number of men and women. One month later, the age category showed 2,000 more men advertising than women. Six months later, men's ads outnumbered women's by 3,000.

While many people over 50 are computer-savvy, some are not quite up to speed. For those who still associate screen names with movie stars, there is no time like the present to learn about computers and Internet dating. Take a class from your local community college or public library and you'll have a chance to meet new people while you learn. If you prefer print media, you can place ads in magazines, newspapers, local and religious publications.

Personal ads: The pluses

- Advertising is an efficient way of reaching large numbers of like-minded people. You'll meet more eligible singles by placing one ad than you could by attending countless concerts, exhibits, and church suppers. Sure, you might meet your dream partner in the grocery line, where Laura met Kofi, but that sort of serendipity is rare. Scanning ads is a more profitable use of your time and energy.
- You get better value compared to other search methods. Matchmaking services charge thousands of dollars, if they agree to take you at all. Cruises and singles-only vacation packages are expensive. While singles' activities and clubs cost less, there is an emotional price to pay for participating in potentially discouraging endeavors. Ads are less costly and often free. Plus, you can scan the personals while lounging at home, comfortable and on your own time.
- You can choose from dozens of websites and hundreds of publications. Every site has its own ambience, each publication its own image. Even the shyest or most particular person can find an appealing venue.

- You're in control. You answer whomever you please on your own schedule. You meet when you're ready. When you lose interest, you end the contact.
- You're anonymous. You can place and answer ads secure in the knowledge no one will know your name until you choose to divulge your identity.

Personal Ads: The Minuses

- It's possible you'll be overwhelmed. It might take hours for you to wade through ads and decide which ones to answer. Don't be surprised if you receive more responses than you feel you can handle!
- You may be deceived. You've no idea of the legitimacy, true appearance, or character of those who advertise or reply. Any individual can easily create a fictitious or misleading online persona.
- There is no guarantee the other person has the capacity to have the kind of relationship you seek.
- You could get no response. If you place or answer an ad and no one responds, you may feel rejected.
- The process may seem slow. It often takes many exchanges of e-mail messages

or phone calls to determine if you want to meet.

- It can be expensive. Some publications and dating sites are free, but others charge membership fees. You may also incur additional costs, for instance, hiring a photographer to take a flattering picture for you to post or paying several dollars a minute to 900 numbers. In the commercial world, romance is a profitable business.

Getting started

As with all the methods for finding a companion described in this book, flexibility and persistence are the keys. Don't give up too soon. Experiment to find out what works best.

If you like to feel chosen, advertising and waiting for responses may suit you better than answering ads. If you want more control, selecting the ads to answer may be your preference. Unless you have a strong bias, try both methods and see how it feels. Test each technique many times before declaring your preference.

Your best strategy is to assume volume is a key to success. Place ads in more than one venue. Select several Internet dating sites or publications. Assess responses or lack of replies. Be ready to change the text or photo, if you don't like the results, and run the ad again.

When replying, send the same message to various advertisers and gauge the reactions. Experiment with variations, eliminate some facts and add others. Craft some responses with great care. Answer other ads quickly, in a light and spontaneous tone. If you get tired or bored, take a break, focus on friends and other activities for a while, and return to your search refreshed.

It helps to have a plan. Keep a notebook and record:

- Dating sites you tried on the Internet
- Dating sites you want to try in the future
- Examples of appealing, funny and clever ads
- Newspapers, magazines, and newsletters in which you've advertised
- Newspapers, magazines, and newsletters for future ads
- List of absolute negative qualities. (Use this list to avoid temptation. For example, suppose you've stated that you'll not date a married person. Should you

connect with someone perfect in every aspect, except you suspect he's got a wife, reread your list of nonnegotiable qualities and move on.)

- List distasteful characteristics. (When you read those key words in an ad or in a reply, you'll not waste time or be tempted to respond. For instance, you do not want to start a family. Or date someone who's currently unemployed or looking for financial support. Don't worry about being specific. There are more than enough people searching the ads to meet your desires.)
- Keep records of those who respond:
  Name:
  Age:
  Positive qualities:
  Geographic location:
  Questions to ask in the future:
  Next contact planned:
  General impression:

Staying motivated

By 50, most of us have had our share of disappointments. A history of failed relationships or losses can make even the most cheerful person weary at the thought of starting yet another search. How do you keep yourself motivated along the way?

- Repeat as often as necessary, "I am doing this by choice. No one is forcing me to find romance. I can quit, try another method or forget the whole business and get a dog."
- Find a buddy to share your ups and downs. Compare responses. Keep your eye out for ads or replies your friend might enjoy and pass them along. (Note: there are two schools of thought on this subject. Some men and women cringe in horror at the thought of passing a name to a friend as if the person was a sweater that didn't fit. Others think it's just fine. Early on in my search, I met Mark for coffee. I was put off by his attire: Bermuda shorts, black dress shoes, and white athletic socks. He had many good points: season tickets to the opera, a successful business, and a nice house in a great neighborhood. But I just couldn't face those knobby knees. So I introduced him to my friend, Emily, who was feeling down after a series of disastrous relationships with deceptive men. She and Mark got along so well they were married within a year. I spent the next five years

looking for my match, while they were enjoying the opera and each other.)

- Place an ad with a friend. Divide expenses. Keep the ad general, mentioning mutual characteristics. Sift through the replies and share the wealth.
- Know your cheerleaders. Keep a list of a few sympathetic supporters, people who can boost your spirits when you're feeling down. Keep the number small — you don't want to repeat yourself — and be specific about what you need. Sometimes you might need advice, but other times you just want someone to listen.
- Include someone on your support team who has succeeded at finding a partner through advertising. The friend who says it can't be done, no matter how well-meaning, is not on your side. Avoid listening to stories of failure. It's too much like hearing about the horrors of surgery just before having an operation.
- Repeat: "This is not a full-time job." Seeking a relationship should be like adding spice to a dish you're cooking. A little is fine; too much overwhelms. Answer ads, check voice mail or e-mail at comfortable intervals, once a day or three

times a week. Having too many interactions at one time dilutes the experience.

- Read the success stories printed in publications or posted on websites. You can get some good ideas for your own search.

Looking for love? Or friendship?

When we know our needs and limitations, we can make wise choices that lead to happy outcomes. It is helpful to know how much intimacy you can stand. Maybe you've never sustained a relationship for longer than a year. Or, despite enjoying a flirtatious e-mail exchange, you feel reluctant to meet your pen pal in person. Better to accept this and pass on advertisers looking for lifetime bonding. Instead, accept your limitations, seek the best e-pal and enjoy.

As middle-aged adults, we recognize friendships can be pursued with less intensity and intoxication than romances, thus allowing us to forgo some of life's drama. On the plus side, friendships are more likely to endure, carry fewer expectations, and offer a better prospect for long term mutual benefit and satisfaction.

E-Searching

By the time this book is published, many thriving dating sites will be defunct and others will have taken their place. Sites funded by advertisements may go under if products don't sell. Those supported by subscriber fees must reach a critical mass or go to the dot-com burial ground.

Small independent sites are often purchased or merged with larger companies. For example, Gifted Professional Singles Network accessed at gpsn.com directs your to "Senior Singles" which gives you access to the very active Match.com. Love@AOL.com and Love.Netscape.com also take you to Match.com.

Sometimes a website exists in name only. You type in the name of one site but then find yourself referred, through a series of links, to another site. For example, you decide to check out Matesearch.net/50UP.htm, because of the term "50up." (Take care to use upper case letters when typing "UP." The seemingly insignificant error of typing "up" in lower case will take you to a pornographic site instead.) Instead of an actual site however, you're linked to <u>One-and-Only.com</u>, a large general dating site, which then sends you to <u>SeniorFriendfinder.com</u>. Although it may seem like a nuisance, this process takes only a few minutes and has the advantage of giving you access to more people.

See what you can find by entering key words such as "personals," "matchmaker" or "dating service" at your search engine. To refine your search, include a modifier such as: "over 50," "mature," or "older." See page 390 for a more comprehensive list of websites,

---

Many publications and Internet sites create sections for advertisers seeking only correspondents or friends. Here you have an opportunity to learn about people living in a different city or culture, find someone who is willing to listen to your woes or your success stories. It can be easier to connect with a person unseen and living far away. Although e-friends have limits, friendly associations can enhance your life while you wait to find romance.

David was thrilled by his e-mail connection with Amy. She was smart and funny and they had mutual interests in politics and nature. They exchanged life histories, holding nothing back, and spent hours writing to each other. She responded to his messages within minutes, yet kept putting off meeting him in person. When they finally met, David thought they hit it off, but Amy declined a second date. David was disappointed and hurt, but he eventually realized Amy was simply more comfortable connecting in cyberspace than in the real world.

Truth in advertising

The anonymity that is so attractive about the Internet is also one of its great dangers. People advertising don't have to be honest. A woman may describe herself as elegant, vivacious and youthful. But when you call her on the phone, she's so depressed she can barely keep up her end of the conversation. A man says he's between jobs but he's actually been collecting disability due to mental problems for years. While these people should not be condemned as outright liars, they were certainly stretching the truth. It is up to you to take every statement with a grain of salt.

There is undeniable emphasis on youth, money and weight in the online world. A survey of Internet ads shows most men and many women in their 70s or 80s want a companion two to ten years younger. Women are often looking for men who are "financially secure," while men want women who are "slim."

Yet often people with high standards can develop a satisfying relationship with someone who does not correspond to their ideals. Suppose you are not so slim and you're ten years older than the top of the advertiser's range. Should you respond anyway?

It's clear a woman over 50 should pass on the ad of a man hoping to start a family. But a woman of average weight could take a chance and respond to a man seeking someone slim, since the meaning is in the eye of the beholder.

Issues of geographic preference, family commitment, and lifestyle habits are difficult to negotiate in midlife. One of my clients, Lois, found this out the hard way. A retired hospital administrator, she enjoyed an active life in Washington D.C., filled with friends, dinner parties, and lots of shopping. She met Tom through an ad in the *Washingtonian Magazine* and was attracted to his humor and good looks. He was about to retire from a lifetime career as an engineer and wanted to move back home to the Oregon coast. Lois thought it sounded like a great adventure. Her kids were grown and she had nothing keeping her in D.C. Or so she thought.

Within a year they were married and living in a small beach town in Oregon. But Lois was miserable. She and Tom quarreled all the time, often about how much time she spent on the phone talking to her friends and family and her frequent trips back East to visit them. When she came to see me, she was depressed. She hadn't realized how much she needed the energy and excitement of a big city in order to thrive.

Eventually Lois moved back to D.C. and rented a small apartment. For a while, she and Tom kept their relationship going by joking about how they had both a beach house and a pied-a-terre in the big city. But it became clear neither was really comfortable in the other's milieu and they split up, amicably.

A picture worth a thousand words

While you can opt for a text-only ad at Internet dating sites, photo ads receive more attention. A visual image gives the advertiser an extra dimension, plus it provides the viewer with all the cues (both good and bad) one gets from physical appearance.

Tony, a fit 66-year-old and the owner of a construction business, was looking for a woman his own age. He liked the idea of spending time with someone who had experienced certain pivotal events, like the birth of rock and roll, at the same time he did. But when he looked at pictures of 66-year-old women on web sites, they usually looked too old to him. Until he saw Sandy's picture. She had an open, smiling face and wore a big hat, tilted over one eye. "I answered that ad because of her hat," Tony says.

Many ads carry no images. Some men and women prefer to make their connection through words alone. They believe personality is more important than appearance in creating a strong relationship. If you're not comfortable including a picture, try your luck with words. Just be open to the possibility of including a photograph, if you're not getting the response you want.

If you do decide to post an image, don't use a driver's license photo or a snapshot from your 1970s album. Also don't use a retouched or glamorized portrait. You will have to face the truth the moment you meet. Lies, whether visual or verbal, are difficult, if not impossible, to explain. Why risk starting a relationship on a dishonest note?

Jon agreed to meet Helen after viewing a picture of her at the web site where she promoted her self-help books. But the photo had been taken nearly twenty-five years earlier and was one of those soft-focus shots that made her look even younger. He was shocked to see how old she appeared when they met in person and fled after about twenty minutes. Perhaps if she had been honest earlier, the discrepancy would not have been so jarring

Choose a recent image that sends the message that you are friendly, accessible and fun to meet. If you use a snapshot taken by a friend, make sure the picture is sharp and well-composed. If you appear too far in the distance, it defeats the purpose and suggests you don't want people to get a good look at you. If it's a shot of you with your grandchildren, this implies being a grandparent is your major role. Instead of using a shadowy image to hide signs of age and excess weight, use a photo emphasizing the features you know others admire.

Consider hiring a professional photographer. It's well worth the expense. Ask for a repeat sitting if you're not satisfied with the results and make sure you get your picture in digital format. Today's digital cameras produce Internet-ready images or you can have your film developed and put on a compact disc, ready to submit.

Men: avoid sloppy clothing, messy hair, undershirts, torn shirts, or, worse, no shirt. Women: too much jewelry and makeup are unappealing. If a website permits more than one image, use photos of yourself in various settings.

Don't:

- Post a photo with other people in it. Don't stand next to a handsome son or daughter whose looks will dazzle the viewer. You want all the attention on you!
- Don't say much about looks if you're going to use a picture. Better to let the viewer decide if they like what they see.
- You should be the focus of the picture. Don't confuse your viewer with scenery or objects in the background that distract.
- Don't use a picture where you appear to have red eyes, an effect created by the reflection of the camera's flash. You can

eliminate this common flaw by asking your photo developer for help.
- Don't use a picture from a few decades ago. Your viewer will recognize those bell-bottoms!

Sometimes men select photos of themselves with their arms around one or two young, attractive women — their daughters or nieces. As seductive as this image may be, it sends the wrong message. Other men might be impressed but middle-aged women aren't looking for a man who advertises his appeal to younger women.

Ted took a different approach when Molly asked him for a photograph. He sent a picture of himself dressed in a T-shirt and shorts holding a large furry animal with a pointed nose and a curly tail. At first, Molly was put off by his bushy beard and large belly but she was intrigued by the unusual animal. When she asked Ted what it was, he explained it was a coatimundi and the picture was taken on one of the tours he leads to South America. This personal story helped Molly decide Tom was an interesting man who she wanted to know better.

Sometimes when you respond to an ad, your correspondent requests a photo before agreeing to meet with you. This person may be focused on appearance or maybe she just wants to see your face so she can recognize you at the coffee shop. Once asked, it's best to comply. Refusing to send your picture after making an initial connection usually suggests you have something to hide.

If you mail a photo, use an actual snapshot rather than a color copy made on a reproduction machine. Dating is supposed to be personal. You don't want to make it look like you're engaged in mass marketing.

Dating on the Internet

According to the *New York Times*, July 23, 2000, ". . . 61% of singles will look for a date on the Internet this year." Online research firm Media Metrix says the number of people using Internet dating sites increased from 3.4 million in 1999 to 5 million in 2000. By the time you're reading this, this number should be substantially larger.

While some websites cater to specific age groups, most appeal to users spanning several decades. Select a site that carries many personal ads in the age range of your interest.

Each site has its own ambience. Most offer additional features such as advice on relationships, success stories from members, chat rooms, and information on vacations, finance, health and improved communication. Some give a sense of community, creating the feeling you've entered a place where you can visit and chat with congenial members. Others are more straightforward: you log on, check your responses and then sign off.

You will find an incredible variety of websites. At some, kinky postings are scattered among the more no-nonsense, romantic ads. Some sites display photos of men and women who look like models. Others display photos so tiny it's unlikely even their mothers would recognize their child. Keep an open mind as you browse websites. Even if a site is uninviting at first, you may find it has features you like after you've spent some time becoming familiar with its resources. Identify, then revisit sites that pique your interest.

Some websites offer helpful tools, for instance, giving you advice on key words to use to find people who match your preference in age and location. When you're ready to respond to an ad, you select a nickname to protect your identity at most sites. You can remain anonymous until you're ready to make contact via personal e-mail, written letter, or telephone. Some sites provide features, such as "hot lists" in which you can keep track of contacts and messages.

At dating sites, members present their information in profile format. Some profiles include a photo or two, others do not. Some sites help you develop your own profile by asking useful questions, for example: How important is religion in your life? Would you accept a companion not interested in sex? How do you spend your day? Other sites ask for your response to frivolous questions which I believe are more distracting than helpful. For example, knowing which movie star you prefer to be trapped with on a desert island doesn't tell me much about your ability to sustain a loving relationship.

When filling out a profile, take your time and answer as many questions as possible but don't agonize over the process. You're trying to find a date, not get security clearance to work for the C.I.A. Chances are your reader will not be scrutinizing every word, reading between the lines to discern your secret thoughts. Don't strain to be humorous. If a light answer comes easily, fine. Avoid silly or excessive messages unless you want a silly person to respond.

Costs differ. Some sites offer a free trial period before you pay. Others allow you to peruse the personal ads, but you can't respond to an advertiser unless you pay a fee. Others require payment just to enter. Generally, fees run about $10–$20 a month; some offer discounted packages for a longer-term commitment. Specialized websites can be expensive; for example, Astrology.com charges $175 for a month's search to find your starmate. While you can experiment with free sites, keep in mind, fee-based sites attract a more serious clientele. A list of recommended sites appears at the back of this book.

Personal ads in print

The popularity of personal ads reached a high in the 1970s, when newspapers, magazines and newsletters competed for market share. Originating in big-city underground weeklies, where offbeat people sought off-center connections, personal ads now appear in *Harvard Magazine*, the

New York Review of Books, religious publications, and specialty magazines. Eight-page neighborhood newsletters display personal ads next to notices for baby sitting and hauling trash.

Fees vary from no cost to hundreds of dollars. Options such as using bold typeface and enclosing the ad in a box add expense. Some publications offer a fee-based mail box for responses which are forwarded at timely intervals. A 900-number and voice mail reply can run up to $2.00 per minute depending on where you live.

Some personals sections are run by syndicates. NVS Interactive Media, in business since 1990, manages ads in 450 to 600 publications around the country. Although it does not track the specific age of users, the company is aware of the large over-50 market. Some publications carry a specific senior section, where the average advertiser age is over 70. But NVS staff say most seniors often don't want to be identified that way and prefer to appear with the general age mix.

The best sites for written ads are local newspapers, neighborhood newsletters, nationally circulated magazines with a specific clientele, book supplements, and free weekly papers. Due to constant changes, a paper carrying ads today may eliminate its personals section tomorrow. Spend time at the newsstand to learn what is current. I've included a few ideas in the sidebar on the next page, as an illustration to spark your own creativity in finding the venue that's right for you.

Ideas for getting the most from your ad

- Your ad might attract more attention if it runs in a publication that carries fewer ads or appears in a novel location such as a small town paper in a different state.
- Peruse newspapers from around the country and abroad. Check out their personals. Call the 800-number or e-mail for more information about readership before placing an ad.
- Contact a publication that does not carry personals, about running your ad in their classifieds. For example, should the *Anchorage Daily News* take your personal ad, it might be read by many interested singles.
- Placing ads can be less costly than answering them. Check out holiday promotions like "Just-in-time-for-summer" or "Valentine's special," which often offer one-time-only placement of a free ad.

Print Ads

Publications come in all flavors. Here are some examples drawn from hundreds of options. Use this list as a stimulus to spark your own list of venues that will work for you.

- *Albuquerque Journal* and the *Albuquerque Tribune*. Both offer a special section, "Mature Life," including personal ads and articles on senior romance.
- *Washingtonian*. Most men and women who place ads are over 50. The average age of the reader is 51. The cost for a 30-word ad is about $90 for a onetime run. Although the staff do not tally phone responses received, they do know that about 15 letters arrive per mailbox. Although declining in popularity over the years, this is still a favorite venue for capitol residents and beyond. In the June 1996 issue, 9 $^1/_2$ pages of ads appeared; the December 2000 issue carried 4 pages of ads.
- *Harvard Magazine*. The median age of readers (both alumni and non-University) is 49. Averaging eight responses

per advertiser, this publication has remained popular over the years and carries four pages of ads per issue. A typical ad runs $200 with an extra $25 mail forwarding fee. Ads also appear simultaneously on the magazine's website: HarvardMagazine.com for an additional $25.

- *New York Review of Books*. The average age of readers is 53. Ads cost $5/word and are witty, intelligent and receive considerable response. One woman who wrote, "Pretty woman will return sexual favors for dog walking of large poodle. Both blonde," caught the attention of a reporter from the *Paris Review* as well as many canine enthusiasts. Buy the print version or check out the personals in the classified section of the online version at nybooks.com.

- When placing a classified, chat with the person taking your information. Inquire about the volume of advertisements the paper handles, the number of older advertisers, and the names of additional sites for ads. If the ads are managed by a syndicate, ask if your notice can be placed in more than one publication.

- Some papers run a "senior section." Don't turn your nose up at this option.
- Look for advertisements about singles' activities, matchmakers, and support groups appearing near the personals. You may get some new ideas for social opportunities and services.
- Find out if the paper offers the services of an "ad writing expert."
- Try advertising in a religious periodical, even if you have a different belief system. Be sure to state your spiritual bent so you won't create false expectations. Many of the magazine's readers may be willing to date someone with a different spirituality.
- Find out if your ad can appear online. Many publications offer both formats, giving you double exposure.
- Brave the classiest publication your finances permit, like *New York Review of Books* or *London Review of Books*. If you find the price of advertising staggering, think about answering ads in these publications.
- Explore enterprises that help you write and place your ad and those that screen responses. Negotiate the best possible price for these services.

Personal Services

Although not specific for subscribers over 50, these reputable services have been in business for years and attract members in an older range. Try:

- Art Lovers' Exchange has been linking unattached lovers of the arts since 1985. Nationwide. (800) 342–5250; <u>alxdating.com</u>.
- Classical Music Lovers' Exchange — for unattached music lovers since 1980. Nationwide. (888) 408-CMLE; <u>cmle.com</u>.
- The Right Stuff announces that "Smart is Sexy" and offers the opportunity for university graduates to meet. (800) 988-5288; <u>rightstuffdating.com</u>.
- Single Booklovers is reached by writing to Box 74, Swarthmore, PA 19081, calling (800) 773-3437, or visiting <u>singlebooklovers.com</u>.

Protect yourself

Although they may fudge a little on pounds and years, most people who place and respond to personal ads are legitimate.

Still you never know. Your correspondent may be writing from his suburban house encircled by flowers and grandchildren or from a backwoods cabin surrounded by attack dogs and weapons.

Luckily the Internet makes it easy to check up on people. If a person responding to your ad arouses suspicion, check him out on Checkmate1.com. This fee-based service provides information on your potential sweetie's credit report, possible aliases, property owned, and names of relatives. Although arrest records are not included, you can get them from CrimCheckInc.com. Learn more about safety when writing and responding to ads in Chapter Five.

While you may approach this venture honestly, others may not be as ethical. Ask as many questions as you can think of before you meet. Do you have common acquaintances? Although this isn't a job interview, can your date offer any references? Even with careful questioning, you can't find out everything. One friend agreed to meet with a man who said he was a doctor at a local hospital. She verified his employment at the hospital but didn't learn until later that he was a janitor, not a doctor.

It's important to do as much checking as you can. If your potential date only provides a business or cell phone number, he may be married. Ask for a home phone number and call him during the early evening. If you feel any concerns, voice them directly and follow up with research. You are the only one who can look out for your own safety and well being.

Success story

Meeting someone by advertising and responding to personal ads can be difficult. It's time-consuming, sometimes expensive, and may end in disappointment and rejection. But your odds of meeting the right person improve dramatically when you broaden your search to include all the potential singles you can reach through ads rather than in person. And you are somewhat less vulnerable during the sorting out process, since it's an impersonal medium.

To the amazement of her friends, Judy, a retired high school teacher, persevered for three years in her quest to find a mate through personal ads. Long after others would have become given up, Judy persisted. Sometimes she took a break, when she was feeling discouraged, but she always returned to the process, eventually widening her scope so she was placing ads in her local mainstream paper, the local alternative paper, her church's newsletter, her cousin's church's newsletter, and her best friend's synagogue newsletter. She sorted through 372 responses, and went on over a hundred coffee dates, before she met Rick, a nice, overweight, retired accountant who just happened to be her dream man.

❮❮ 4 ❯❯

The Whole Truth and Nothing But

Good advertising copywriters enjoy six-figure salaries on Madison Avenue. If you're not a professional copywriter, it can be scary to sit down and write an ad — especially to promote yourself. You may never be a Madison Avenue copywriter, but you can still learn to write a winning ad.

This chapter provides tips on how to write your own ad and what to look for when you're responding to ads. Just as you should be thoughtful about what you say and how you say it, you should take seriously what the advertiser requests. If he seeks a woman with certain physical characteristics, believe it. If you don't fit the request, forget it. Better to answer the ad of someone with whom you at least have a chance.

This chapter will help you avoid pitfalls

and provide suggestions to convey important information. Below are guidelines for composing a successful advertisement. When starting to write, please reread the suggestions so they'll be fresh in your mind.

Finding the right words

Begin by reading the ads already posted at the venue of your choice. Also scan ads at other sites. Don't try to reinvent the wheel. Identify ads that sound good and might work for you. Just like an artist, look to others for inspiration. Imitation isn't plagiarism.

Copy must be tailored to meet the individual needs of the advertiser. Write to convey your most appealing qualities. Ads work best when they say more about you and less about who you are seeking. You want to appear discerning and thoughtful, but you could easily discourage a potential match if your requirements are too strict.

Of course you have the right to ask for the moon, but it doesn't mean your request will be fulfilled. There are some basics you might state. If you want to have a second family, say it. If you prefer to date someone of a certain religion or someone with sufficient free time to accompany you on your travels, be clear.

Be as flexible as possible, but know yourself and your standards. In a newspaper ad, where every word counts, you'll want to choose the most vital and vivid. If you're writing a profile for a web site, you have more room to describe yourself and your preferences. Below are some important issues you will want to consider.

- Reveal your age? Better to either state your age, which will be found out soon enough, or say nothing. Here's where your photo is worth a thousand words.
- Be flexible in your age preference. Hugh Hefner at 77 lives with a girlfriend who is 23 and seven other women in their twenties. But those of us who don't have his wealth and fame, are not likely to attract partners who are so much younger. Be realistic when you advertise. When answering ads, don't discount a woman or man because he or she is younger or older than you'd prefer. Remember, if you find the contents appealing, you'll soon forget about the packaging.
- Don't put much weight on weight. Fewer

people are interested in weight than you might think. First of all, don't lie. If you can describe yourself accurately with adjectives like slim, athletic, slender, petite, wiry, fit, flab-free, trim, thin, or willowy, so much the better. "Height and weight proportional" has lost its punch. If you're average weight then try something a little quirky to get your message across: "My height and weight are normal, like the rest of me." Or: "I weigh neither too much nor too little." If you're heavy by usual standards, you're not going to be able to hide the fact when you meet. Present the information up front. "Not slim" is a fine way of saying you're not slim. You might also use words like solid, Rubenesque, heavy or weighty. You can say, "Weight is not an issue . . . for me!" and let the reader decide if is an issue for him. Please believe me when I say that there are plenty of men and women who don't care about weight.

- Reveal your height. If the profile asks for your height, give it. There's no way to disguise your height when you meet.
- Be honest about your minimum standards regarding appearance. If looks are important to you, feel no shame. You can say "no fatties (or anorexics) need

apply." Another place where pictures are so important.

- Consider employment status. Are you currently unemployed or "between jobs?" If you're a consultant, exactly what kind of consulting? If you're fortunate enough to have free time, describe how you spend it. "I'm a consultant with my own accounting business which gives me time to study French and ride my bike." Notice I say *fortunate*. This isn't the place to talk about your hours being cut in favor of a younger employee or your business failing. State your own employment status with phrases such as "financially secure" or "successful lawyer" or "teacher with a 20-year service award." Keep in mind that people seeking others with financial resources may be a bit shaky financially. It's up to you to do the screening.
- Consider health issues. Health concerns can be significant for those over 50. Do you have health issues someone should know about in advance? If you're a wheelchair user, you might want to tell this up front but your ad isn't the place to detail your heart condition or prostate troubles. Some people like to proclaim their STD status but, as valuable as this

information might be, I feel it's un-appealing to broadcast this intimate detail to people you haven't yet met.

- State your preference regarding family involvement. Define your attitude toward the prospect of new children in your life. You might decide you're finished with raising a family and have no desire to date someone who has family obligations, whether the kids are young or already grown. Both men and women over 50 can have teenage or even younger children from a previous relationship. On the other hand, a lifelong bachelor might be thrilled by the prospect of an instant family. And a woman who hasn't had much success with her own children might welcome the opportunity to be a stepparent.

- Resist the urge to mention pets, relatives, children and grandchildren. At most, limit your reference to "caring grandparent" and let it go at that. Or you might say "My grown children are special to me but are self-sufficient and have their own lives." Your message should focus on what you offer a potential companion.

- Omit your family problems. Suppose the reality is you have a pack of family troubles. You have difficult children or elderly parents in your charge. Don't advertise your woes. If you're in this situation and you're replying to ads, look for someone who mentions his kind, tolerant or sympathetic nature.

- Determine how much adventure you'd like in your life. Are you looking for a retiree who's available for local activities? Are you still working, but would like a companion for vacations? Be clear about your preferences.
- Reveal your level of interest in activities. If you like hiking, climbing, and marathon running, say it. You'll eliminate those with more sedentary interests. If you want nothing more adventurous than garage sales and read an ad requesting a companion to trek in Nepal, move on.
- Leave out the loneliness. Advertising your state of loneliness is unattractive at best, distasteful at worst. You'll discourage all but the neediest readers. If this indeed is the state you find yourself in, don't mention it. The person who answers your ad will find out soon enough if you aren't able to camouflage your forlorn condition.
- Interests are important. Be proud of your passions and commitments — they help define you and attract others with the

same interests. Like to travel? State your interest and mention a favorite place, but don't offer an itinerary. If you have a lot of pursuits, don't write a list — lists make dull reading. Instead pick three diverse pastimes such as "Likes opera, cooks great Thai food, and hikes on weekends." Here's an example I took from an actual ad: "Warm-blooded woman, 61, seeks friend to share early asparagus, late Beethoven, good books, and other fine things." Suppose your main interests are all outdoors. You're much more likely to capture your reader's attention by saying, "I like the outdoors," instead of listing: "kayaking, fishing, hiking, white water rafting, rock climbing, etc." Assuming you're looking for that special someone who shares your passions, be specific. If you like music, mention a composer. Don't make a long list of your favorite songs or movies, mention only one or two.

- Don't mention sex. No matter how much you enjoy sex, any allusion, no matter how vague, has no place in your ad. Unless, of course, you want to attract a person for whom sex is the priority. Conveying that you're sexy and attractive must be done in an understated way, otherwise you may be deluged by requests for lovemaking. Likewise, you may read plenty of ads both from men and women who advertise sexual interest or prowess. If this is what you want, that's fine. If not, don't answer an ad featuring sex. You're not going to divert the advertiser from his or her main interest no matter how smart and charming you are.

- If religion is important, state your preference. This is an area unlikely to change.
- Consider your relationship preference. Maybe you're widowed and can't imagine ever getting married again. "Seeks companionship" is vague, but appropriate. On the other hand, what if marriage is your goal? Try using "seeks stable relationship." "Long-term" will also work, but is becoming a cliché. Remember, you can ask for what you want but there's no guarantee you will get it. Don't rule out the possibility that your desires or those of your dates might change over time. Still it's best to provide information on what you're currently seeking.
- Forget past relationships. Make no mention of what sort of husband you were in the past, how much you loved your deceased wife, or the pain you suffered at

the hands of your ex. No mention of how happy you were in former times nor how miserable. No, no, no.

- It's not what you're not. Some people advertise that they're not a stalker, a needy person, a loner. Such statements simply raise those unpleasant images in the reader's mind. They certainly don't calm their apprehensions. Stick to the positive.
- Advertise who you are. Describe the qualities that make you unique. This can be tough to do on your own, so enlist a friend's help. Don't exaggerate or undersell. Create a catalogue of applicable adjectives and activities. I was asked by my friend, Susan, to help with this task and came up with, "Not your average redhead." Ambiguous, but accurate. Susan has nifty red-orange hair and no one would consider her average anything. Two men answered her ad. She married one.
- Say what you're seeking. Change negatives to positives. If you don't want someone who's abusive or has a temper, you might advertise for someone who's kind or mild mannered.
- Avoid vagueness. These days the notion of being "spiritual" is too vague. If you mean honest, ethical, or religious then

say so. Find a word to replace "affectionate." This suggests either sexuality or how a pet behaves. "Open" or "caring" is a better choice. Don't use "whatever," as in this statement: "I'd like to meet someone for companionship by e-mail, phone or *whatever*." This statement is more informative: "I'd like to meet someone with whom I can e-mail, chat on the phone or share a cup of coffee."

- Avoid synonyms in the ad, for example, "honest" and "sincere." Use one or the other. A single word has more punch.
- Resist forced humor. Don't make jokes. Be lighthearted, but not silly.
- Be as specific as you can. When describing employment, don't say "professional." This could be shorthand for professional thief or professional sumo wrestler. Likewise "self-employed" requires elaboration. Instead of saying you're retired, be specific or mention what you're doing currently, for instance, "Retired schoolteacher who spends my time mentoring teens" or "a retired schoolteacher taking classes in Italian and archaeology."
- Use the prompts at websites for inspiration. Some websites offer prompts to elicit the information you'd like to

convey. Use the prompts to help write a better ad.

- Use phrases or short sentences. You don't need to write in complete sentences and certainly not in paragraph format. Short sentences, even sentence fragments, are acceptable in personal ads.

- Avoid overused words that have lost their punch as well as their meaning, for instance: soul mate, professional, playful, irreverent, quality relationship, etc. (That's right: don't use "etc." it's presumptuous to leave the reader to fill in the blanks. The reader doesn't know you and won't have the fuzziest notion of what you mean when you say, "Likes to read, garden, etc.".) Avoid the word, "average." No one wants to be thought of as middle-of-the-road. Avoid the phrase "wonderful children" when describing your family. Also, "love" is overused. Instead of "loves to garden" how about "enthusiastic gardener" or "unstoppable gardener" as a quirkier way of getting your point across. Forget "people-person." This phrase went out two decades ago. Try, "I'm outgoing." "Semiretired" is a tired phrase. Don't use the word "adorable" to describe your

100

grandchildren, your iguana or yourself under any circumstances.

- Eliminate clichés. Don't mention walks on the beach or fireside cuddles to give an impression of romance. They say nothing about your genuine capacity for it.
- Omit comparisons. There are opposing opinions on whether to say that you resemble a famous person. On one hand it might be helpful for the reader to get a glimpse of your type. Alternatively, you don't want to hint that answering your ad will deliver Robert Redford to Starbucks for coffee.
- Be descriptive, not evasive. Add a word or two that suggests more of a description. Instead of saying "brown hair" write "shoulder-length brown hair." Instead of grey hair, try silver. You don't need the adjectives in "early 60s" or "late 70s."
- Adjectives to use: honest, affectionate, friendly, good listener, happy, passionate, gentle, stable, spirited, expressive, active, enthusiastic, energetic, trustworthy, kind, responsible, adventurous, committed, smart, spontaneous, intense, forgiving, quick, smiling, resilient, supportive. "Very bright" while it might turn off some will attract others. "High main-

tenance" could be a turnoff for many but a challenge for some.

- Use adjectives sparingly. Four in a row is maximum. A string of adjectives (like the one above) loses punch.
- Emphasize the positive. Let your reader know if you're nondemanding, have a sense of humor or can truly say that you're "youthful, positive and cheerful."
- Unmentionables: Avoid overly-charged requests or those impossible to fulfill. If you advertise for someone "not married," you imply past problems. Don't request someone "noncritical." It's not humanly possible. "All replies answered so what do you have to lose?" sounds desperate. Don't say you "need" something — it sounds too . . . well, needy.
- Less is more. Eliminate any unnecessary words. Ask a friend to read your ad or seek the services of an editor. Call your local university. You may find a graduate student in the English department willing to edit your ad for a fee. Or call your local community college or adult education program; students in editing classes will often edit, sometimes without a charge, to build up their portfolios. Make your ad succinct, even if you're permitted an unlimited amount of space.

- Don't cut down your options: Saying you want someone who can "keep up" with you might scare away a perfectly nice person who prefers quieter activities. Don't mention your "interest in dining out." You might eliminate someone on a fixed income or someone who loves whipping up five-course gourmet meals at home.
- Proofread before posting. Don't expect the venue to proofread your ad. Awkward grammar and spelling mistakes will discourage discerning readers.

Your personal ad is not the place to be brutally honest about your quirks and foibles. Your goal is to attract someone. Flowers use all sorts of strategies to attract the creatures that pollinate them, including color, scent, and shape. Likewise, you want to present the most vivid, vital, and outstanding picture of yourself in your ad.

Eye-catching headlines

Use your headline as a "hook" to get the reader interested. Check out other ads to see what catches your eye.

Avoid standard abbreviations unless

space is at a premium. Use "unattached" rather than SWM; replace ISO with "seeks." Remember: A simply written headline is more forceful than one cluttered with words.

Here are some good examples:

- **Bluegrass, Blues & NPR** — the writer mentions varied music interests and hints at social and political values by mentioning an intellectually oriented radio station.
- **60s Seeking 60s** — says it like it is.
- **I live at Barnes and Noble** — from a woman who likes to read. Her use of the word "I" works in this example but in most cases your headline will have more punch if you leave it out.
- **Adventurous but responsible** — presents an attractive image of contrasts.
- **Holding all the cards but one** — written by someone who goes on to say that the one card missing is romance.
- **I promise no dull moments** — written by a 79-year-old woman. It's unexpected and it works.
- **Not looking for Mr. Perfect** — an appealing use of a negative request; conveys humility and realistic expectations.

- **Boston-based writer/academic seeks similar** — conveys exactly who the writer is and what he seeks. This ad will likely discourage any but local scholars, which is fine if that's who the writer wants.
- **Aloha** — a charming headline written by a 59-year-old woman from Hawaii, which signals she is warm, friendly, and open.
- **Just a regular guy looking for an honest and caring woman** — You might think this one is too humble, but it rings of honesty and modesty. The accompanying photo gives the same message.
- **Nerd scientist looking for soul mate** — Normally I cringe at the word soul mate but in this instance (perhaps because of the contrast) I find it irresistible.
- **Sensible but not intellectual** — might be positive for some but make others wonder if your potential date couldn't get a GED
- **I value the ability to drive as well as be a passenger in life** — Nice way to say "we're equals."
- **Looking for terrific friendship** — "Friendship first" is a strong message.
- **Lives richly textured full life** — Think about evocative images. Here we conjure

appealing suggestions of music, woven cloth and, best of all, food!

- **Don't like going out for breakfast and telling the hostess, 'Just one, please.'** — Clear tale told with taste.
- **I have three passions: love of life, love of nature and love of dancing. Could you be my fourth?** — Sweet.
- **Work like you don't need the money, love like you've never been hurt, and dance like nobody's watching** — Plagiarized but worth the try.
- **No baggage except when I travel** — Clever. Hope you mean it if you say it.
- **Don't you just hate the process of dating at this age?** — What a hook! Irresistible!
- **Writer, listener . . .** — My kind of guy.
- **Nautical, but nice** — Describing a sailor.
- **Retired, not tired** — Good headline. "Re-tired" is even more eye-catching.
- **Looking for my new best friend** — Nice thought.
- **Physician/artist/writer** — This was my ad.
- **Youthful version of a 58 year-old** — a fine way of saying this.
- **Not slim** — an honest way of telling it like it is.

In general, choose a headline that fits on one line. For example, "Sleepless in Des Moines" is a nice play on the expression, *Sleepless in Seattle*. Make sure the important words are up front.

Headlines to avoid

I think you'll cringe as you read the headlines below. Refer to this list when writing yours.

- **I'm a smoker, but plan to quit** — don't make promises; just present who you are at the moment.
- **Never been violent or abusive, never could** — disclaimers like this evoke the qualities the advertiser is trying to repudiate
- **I'm liberal, and question the ethical intentions of the current move toward a global economy** — dull
- **Not your usual guy** — guy/gal are weak words.
- **Looking for the impossible** — and doomed to fail
- **Lonely in New Jersey** — sad and unpromising
- **A hug (very often) means a lot . . . at**

least it does to me — written in a clumsy style, seems to hint at a sad past when hugs were given and not received well

- **An ideal relationship is one where we can't keep our hands off of each other** — implies that sexuality is expected and needed. How about waiting to see what evolves instead of being so candid? The writer scares away potential dates shy about sex.

- **Before she likes me, she must like herself** — Waste of words and time.

- **I'm 50 (or 60 or 80) but look and act much younger** — How much younger? Twenty-five? Thirteen? Instead of trying to downplay your age, give examples of your liveliness, for instance, "Enjoys long hikes," or "Willing to try that square dance class," or "Looking for a partner for a tandem bike." Or you could say, as one advertiser did: "I'm a youthful version of a 58-year-old."

- **Is there life out there?** — This ad was accompanied by a photo in which the 71-year old writer looks lively in a strapless blue evening dress with her hair done up nicely. I found the headline irritating. How about: "Would you like to share the good life with me?"

- **I am widowed** or **Happily married for thirty-five years** — bad start to an ad.
- **I have an A to Z personality . . . aloof to zany** — this headline is too cute for my taste but usually it's good to be original. You'll have to decide for yourself.
- **I'm tired of game players and head games** — these terms were vague in the 1970s and haven't become any clearer in this millennium. Besides, this emphasizes the negative rather than the positive.

Choose your handle

You may be asked to choose a short name, a "handle," to identify yourself. This name will appear at a prominent place in your ad and can be used as a form of address by those who respond. Choose a term that is uncomplicated and memorable. Don't select a confusing collection of letters and numbers, a suggestive term, or something excessively cute. Select a first name, nickname or word that describes an interest. Here are some good examples:

- "Serenity Pete" is the screen name of a 68-year-old retired man. It may or may not be his given name, but it's a genuine male name that's not cute or an obvious camouflage and it gives a sense of how he sees himself.

- "A Mensch" is the screen name of a 55-year-old man from New York who uses this Yiddish word to signal his ethnic identity and to convey how he sees himself: as an decent, honest, reliable solid citizen.
- "Beautiful Swimmer" is the screen name of a 50 year old dancer and writer. It appeals because it has a dreamy, artistic quality while also indicating an active life and an attractive appearance.

Long format ads and profiles

Many Internet dating sites offer a set of prompts for users. You're asked questions and given substantial space for your answers. Such disclosure has its advantages

In filling out the questionnaire, you may find some of the questions silly. A favorite is "What's your sign?" If this question annoys you, you might respond "I thought this question disappeared along with bell bottoms and love beads." Or you can just write, "Not important" and leave it at that.

There might be some information you

wouldn't reveal to a good friend — let alone publish on the Internet. For example, one site asks for your romantic/sensual/erotic profile. A formidable question. Here's a possible response: "I can say I'm affectionate . . . and this is as far as I want to go with this question. Get to know me and find out the rest."

If any questions make you uneasy, respond with something gentle, smart or funny. You do not have to reveal anything that makes you uncomfortable.

Short format ads

When entering most Internet dating sites, you'll see a series of ads. Each ad usually includes a picture and a few lines of information. If the reader wants to know more, he or she can click and read further. Some sites allow you to gather more information without subscribing, whereas others request payment. Take note of the advertisements to see how much space you'll have for your information. Write several drafts of your ad until it's concise enough to encourage the reader to respond. You want to put the most attractive and unique words up front to entice the reader to read more.

Men seeking women

As I suggested above, spend some time perusing other ads to see what works and doesn't work for you. In the next two sections, I've given examples of ads placed by men and women, along with my suggestions.

These ads were placed by men, in newspapers, magazines and on Internet dating sites.

Serenity Pete. My favorite artist is John Singer Sergeant; I like Mustang convertibles; Lindbergh is my hero; I like all major authors. I'm loyal, affectionate, fun-loving, gentle. In the past, I was a daring, adventurous soul, now still looking for excitement and adventures and in the future will continue to go for the gusto. Looking for a personable lady . . . witty, humorous with an optimistic attitude . . . not necessarily an athlete . . . but if she can play tennis fine . . . if not, we'll go dancing . . . hopefully, her interests are many . . . we'll share differences as well as similarities . . . open minded to search, learn and make do . . . if the chemistry is there . . . we'll ignite it. There is a lot more to say. If interested, make me smile with a reply.

This charming ad was accompanied by a good quality, studio-type photo of Serenity Pete, smiling and looking pleasant. The Mustang convertible conjures up a snappy image. He lets the reader know his present and future are as significant as his past. His requests are open-ended and he presents himself as honest, telling neither too much nor too little. If I were going to change anything in this ad, I'd advise him to choose one favorite author rather than list "all major authors," and substitute "warm" or "caring" for "affectionate." Also his misspelling of his favorite artist's name makes him appear either ignorant or careless.

Positive, outgoing and gregarious, but I can't bring myself to talk or write about myself. I don't have too many exciting things to tell about. Want to hear more? Send me a note. All messages will be answered as I believe that failure to reply is ill-mannered.

This ad from Paul, a 72-year-old widowed and retired accountant is too vague.

Does Paul want to convey that he's shy? Better to say, "I'm shy but once you get to know me you'll find me a man of action." Rather than say he has nothing exciting to offer, he should tell an anecdote about a trip, his pet, or what happened at his last professional meeting. His promise to answer all replies might be more than he can deliver, although I doubt he got many replies to this ad.

> Active, healthy, humorous, intelligent. Looking for a nice, good looking lady between 57 and 67 years of age. She should be of average build, love grandkids, and want to share everything. Someone to be a lover and a best friend, who would like to travel or take short trips or just stay home and enjoy each other. A nonsmoker and social drinker — in other words someone special.

Don, a 71-year-old rancher from the Midwest, selected four positive words for a great start to his ad. By choosing "active" and "healthy" he conveys that he's not limited by age. His age requirement is narrow, yet not insulting. But his request for a woman who's "nice and good looking" can

Questions to
Kickstart Your Ad Writing

- How would you describe yourself? What color is your hair? Your eyes? Are you tall/short? Average build?
- How about your personality? Are you outgoing, optimistic, quiet, confident, shy? Are you reliable, sympathetic, a good listener? What are your unique/best qualities?
- How do you spend most of your time? At an occupation? A hobby? Traveling? Volunteer activities? Family activities?
- What are your interests? Are you passionate about politics, sports, the arts? Is religion important to you? Do you belong to any groups, clubs or societies? Can you dance? What newspapers/magazines do you read? What music do you prefer? What movies do you like? Do you like to be outdoors or spend the night in front of the TV or computer?
- What level of education do you have? What classes are you taking now?
- What are your likes and dislikes? What foods do you enjoy? Can you cook? What is your ideal night out? What is your least ideal night out?

- Do you have a dog, a cat, a boa constrictor? Do you like pets?
- Do you have children? Are you open to a partner with children?
- Do you have a philosophy of life? Any hopes, dreams, or ambitions?
- What kind of person are you looking for?
- What kind of relationship do you want?
- How far would you travel to meet the right person?

---

be a waste of words. If a woman thinks of herself as attractive, she'll not hesitate to reply. A shy woman who is tentative in her self-appraisal might be discouraged. Who knows how Don defines good looks? These qualities are in the eyes of the beholder. Saying he is looking for women who "love grandkids" is a good way of indicating an important aspect of his life.

I'm a 55-year-old park maintenance supervisor whose most recent exciting experience was fulfilling a dream by taking a world cruise, wisely spending some of the inheritance my mother left me. Physically, I prefer petite, dark-haired, dark-eyed beauties.

The writer's world cruise experience resonates with adventure, but he gives too much financial information, which will attract women who want to help him spend the rest of his inheritance. His specific physical description will make even the most money-seeking women squirm.

I'm a 63-year-old who was duped and treated badly. Unfortunately, sincere persons must tolerate game players on the net. These charlatans choose to live behind their computers, pretending to be someone they're not. I'm not seeking a pen pal in this forum but attempting to sow the seeds of a quality relationship.

The writer neglects to say how he makes a living and starts his ad with a tirade about a previous experience. This is an angry man who was probably genuinely hurt, but an ad is not the place to express this. This entry might attract women who have a great need to rescue someone or who are just as angry about being duped on the Internet. Although unappealing, his honesty might help him find an appropriate match.

I'm a 69-year-old manuscript editor with an interest in dancing and listening to NPR who seeks someone with a strong sense of the endless possibilities life offers. Can we share learning, loving, appreciating the endless ironies of a fickle world? I want to share some great meals and the tender moments they foster.

Very nice request. He offers a good sense of himself through his statements about what he'd like to share.

I am a 67-year-old retired high school teacher who enjoys life. I take every day as it comes and like to keep active. I am very positive in my thinking and look on the bright side of things. I enjoy the sunshine and warm weather. I enjoy the outdoors very much. I like traveling, flying in small or large airplanes, riding my new Harley-Davidson. I enjoy lawn work.

Because of the repeated use of the word "I," the writer sounds self-centered. The ad would carry more punch if it read: "Would you like to share activities that make life fun? Seeking a positive man who enjoys flying, riding motorcycles and warm weather . . ."

I'm a 66-year-old business school professor who just returned from living eight years in Europe. I love opera and am looking for a friend who is agile and bright and creative and cute. If you ever have wanted to have a running partner, I just might be the ticket. Don't worry, I don't run fast.

Cuteness isn't always bad. I find this ad appealing for two reasons. First, the writer lets us know he just returned from abroad and is starting a new phase of his life. Maybe he just ended a relationship and needed to escape to the US, but there's no need to spell this out. Second: he uses humor at his own expense. He's willing to go for a run but recognizes his own limitations. A lady marathoner might not respond, but a woman who is self-conscious about her own athletic abilities might be delighted by his candor and humor.

I'm a 59-year-old truck driver . . . looks aren't important. I want a girl 45 to 57 years old, 5'5" to 5'8" tall, 125 to 165 lbs. Romantic, sensuous, sexy, loving, adventurous, and willing to try new things, and MUST be a one-man woman.

This man says looks aren't important but then is specific in his preferences. He gives no information about his character. The one thing you can be sure of is his interest in sex. He might turn out to be a compassionate and caring man who would make a fine companion, but there's no way of knowing.

Life is about the fine art of sharing. In the end people are who they are and that's who they are supposed to be. It sounds simplistic but most home truths are. The trick of making both yourself and your "other" happy seems to me to enjoy and appreciate them for who and what they truly are and accept that any changes are apt to be minor and short lived. "To thine own self be true," is good advice for both parties in a relationship. If you can give and love and share with the other, and still remain true to yourself, you can create a loving relationship. Certainly seems worth the effort.

This is an excerpt from an ad posted by "A Mensch," the screen name of a 55-year-old man from New York. His ad could use some editing — he could have eliminated many words and still made his point. How about: "To thine own self be true, is good relationship advice. Share, be honest, and don't expect major changes in yourself or your partner."

I'm a 66-year-old man from Texas who prefers encounters and interludes . . . I seek a comfortable buddy who can travel and is good company.

Note the inconsistencies in this ad. Does he want brief encounters or a relationship? Or both? Does he know what he wants? Moral: read and reread your ad and edit out incongruities.

My name is Tommy. I'm a 52-year-old from New Hampshire and I've had a variety of interesting careers.

Too vague. Better to pick one career and tell about it. Better still, describe what you're doing right now. You might say, "After a number of interesting careers, I'm now a librarian in a large law firm, a job which I enjoy." Of course, if you hate it, don't say a word about your distress. Talk about the future instead: "I'm studying to be a social worker and look forward to graduation." If you have nothing good to say about your current job, say nothing and write about how much you like singing with your church choir. Speaking of jobs, don't inflate your current position to make it sound like more than it really is.

I'm a 59-year-old South African man. My children live with me part-time . . . I'm ready for adventure and willing to move.

Think about this excerpt. Would you want to meet a man who's ready to leave his children and move to another continent?

I'm a 53-year-old natural health care worker. I'm considerate, romantic, determined, forgiving and a great cook. I would like to find the love of my life, friend forever. Someone to share the best years of our lives.

Less is more. The writer shows a picture of himself wearing tuxedo with pink boutonniere. Well done.

If you are interested in a friend only, get a good book. If you are interested in a sensual, caring relationship, you have my attention. I will answer all inquiries but insist on a picture. No picture, no answer. And last, but not least: do you solemnly swear the testimony you are about to give is the whole truth?

I found this ad, placed by a 58-year-old retired judge, quite unappealing. Here's a crotchety man making an effort to be humorous, but it doesn't work. He might soften his approach with, "You have my attention if you're looking for a warm and caring relationship. Let's exchange pictures so we can see each other's eyes before we meet. I solemnly swear the testimony I give about being a kind and caring man is the whole truth." This sounds better because he puts the joke on himself rather than the reader.

Women seeking men

As I've scanned several hundred ads placed by women on Internet sites, a common flaw emerges: long, rambling ads filled with vague romantic notions. These ads might be attractive to other women but they're not going to captivate men. While men often limit their options by being too specific about physical preferences, women tend to reveal too much about themselves emotionally.

I'm a 57-year-old retired high school teacher who is feminine, petite and a good listener. I'm looking for a sensitive, kind, fun-loving man who likes to laugh and enjoy life. He would be a considerate gentleman who knows how to treat a lady.

The ad is good until the writer asks for a man who knows how to treat a lady. That can imply almost anything from opening car doors to solid financial support.

What sets me apart from others? I have a great interest in seeing the Mariner's baseball team win. I'm looking for friendship and correspondence.

A winning effort by 71-year-old Mona. She's wise to emphasize an interest likely to be shared with a man. She seeks friendship and correspondence, non-predatory requests. She demonstrates wisdom by making no reference to how much younger she feels or appears. A reader would cringe if she used a phrase such as "I don't look or act my age."

I'm 68 and I was married for along time. We had five children and now I have 10 grandchildren. I divorced my first husband, a dentist and went bankrupt. I remarried and it was awful, but he was a good grandfather. We had nothing in common and he was an uncaring lover and instead of talking he told stupid jokes! I hope I can do better this time.

Of course you wouldn't dream of posting an ad like this. But one woman did.

WWF, 5'4½", 57, brown eyes, shoulder-length brown hair, with a little gray, weigh 180 lbs., speak some French, have a small dog and a doll collection, wear glasses, on the quiet side, and have two grand babies. I do not smoke or drink, am spiritual, can take long walks, and am honest and sensitive. Like male 58–69, intelligent and caring, likes music and movies, preferably average weight. I live in Phoenix.

This writer should have asked a friend or professional editor to eliminate unessential words. And I would advise her to get rid of the reference to the doll collection, a hobby unlikely to dazzle most men. Instead of being so specific in her preferred age range, she could have asked for men 55+, which would eliminate younger men and keep older men on the back burner. She also didn't need to give her exact height (5'4" would be sufficient) and weight — she could have said "solid" or "substantial" or even "I look normal," to get across the idea she's not skinny.

I'm a 50-year-old retired administrative assistant in Chicago who's a little overweight, but I am on a healthy weight loss program and go to a gym three times weekly.

Leave out what you hope will happen in the future. "I'm a regular at my gym," is enough.

I am an attractive 67-year-old fun-loving romantic from Tucson with an affectionate nature who loves to travel. I enjoy watching basketball, sailing, and romantic dinners. I like to try new things and have a happy, optimistic, adventurous spirit. I am easy to talk to and am a good listener. My favorite car is a Lexus and I shop in boutiques in NYC. I make the world's best meatballs.

By stating that her favorite car is a Lexus and she likes to shop in boutiques in NYC, this woman might scare away any man who's not financially secure . . . and generous. If that's what she wants, fine. To her credit, she humanizes the somewhat snobby picture she paints of herself with a great statement about making the world's best meatballs.

Hello Car Buffs. I'm a 1932 Rolls in near mint condition. 4'10" used to be 5'. Low mileage, beautiful interior (exterior isn't bad either)! All original parts, some stabilized! Doesn't run but walks briskly 2+ miles per day, weather permitting! . . . You can be my hero! I think you guys want a woman 20 years younger than yourselves. I'd like Brad Pitt to phone me or perhaps Julio

Iglesias to serenade me while I sip wine by candlelight. They'll tell me I'm beautiful. But the truth is: I am really quite cute! Also petite, loving, understanding, and altogether precious!

What a gutsy ad by a thin and trim 71-year-old woman. One suggestion: leave out the fact she's shrunk two inches. It made me — and will make readers — squirm.

I'm very good looking (formerly breathtaking) and 5'10". I am smart and funny and outgoing. I'm a faithful friend and lover. I love music and dancing and dinner parties and reading and movies and napping and being in love. I hope to find a tall, distinguished gentleman. I hope he is warm and attentive. I hope he likes dinners out, being with friends, having parties, and dancing. I hope he likes to be silly sometimes and serious sometimes. I hope he's a thinker and a reader. I hope he will be romantic, I miss being in love. I had a very creative and exciting business career. I had a perfect marriage to an extraordinary man. Today I have a wonderful lifestyle and many great friends, however, I don't like being a single in the world of couples. I've been a widow for two years and I realize I need a partner again.

Sounds like an interesting 69-year-old woman. But she could have made it much shorter and snappier, for instance: "I'm 5'10" and good looking — formerly breathtaking. My friends find me smart, funny, and outgoing. My interests: music, dancing, reading, napping, and being in love. Looking for a warm and attentive gentleman to share being silly and serious. My life is great but missing that special someone."

I'm a newly divorced 68-year-old art teacher. I really want this new relationship to be my last one. My eyes are a little more open this time than in the past. "Been there, done that" enough times!

The advertiser comes across as wounded and cynical, and thus signals that she is vulnerable to manipulative men.

I'm a 67-year-old woman from a Texas small town. I am very creative; painting and writing are two ways of expressing that creativity. I've had a very interesting life so far; to get the details you'll just have to get to know me. I'm in the process of writing several children's books and plan to illustrate them myself. My central passion is my family. I'm an only child and am very proud of my rather large extended family. We are very close and supportive — which is very important to me. I'm looking for someone who has at least a few of the same likes as I have listed about myself. But, especially someone who is loving — and has no problem showing it — a gentleman. I truly feel that to love and be loved is the most precious gift in one's life.

This ad is far too long and rambling. How about: "Looking for a loving man to share my life. I paint and write children's books. My large, extended family would welcome you! Get to know me and you'll learn more about my interesting life."

I'm a 62-year-old nursing consultant. Would you like a long term relationship filled with unconditional love that knows no boundaries; that accepts one another in all their wonder and celebrates that specialness; that has good communication, emotional intimacy, being best of friends and sharing of life's adventures; honesty and dependability, caring and concern for the benefit of each other and giving back for those things we have been given, playfulness and lots of spontaneous laughter, passion for life and each other? Would you like a gentle, kind, caring and romantic soul with a strong sense of adventure and who is optimistic and wants to explore a love relationship with a young at heart lady?

Another long and rambling ad. I'd suggest: "Nursing consultant seeks to share caring relationship. I'm dependable, passionate and have a great sense of humor. Are you an optimistic man looking for romance with a young-at-heart lady?"

A retired school teacher, very interested in lots of outdoor activities asks for a practical person with real expectations that is not hung up on superficial, materialistic things.

The writer would be better advised to emphasize these aspects of her own personality and let the reader appreciate them. With a little luck, he will have the same qualities.

I'm a 50-year-old social services consultant from the Midwest. Is there anyone out there that REALLY doesn't have emotional baggage??? I don't require much, but honesty, kindness, passion and wit are very important to me. I need someone that is looking for a partner/companion/lover to share time and experiences with. Don't tell me that is what you want if it is really not!!

This ad just can't be fixed. The writer needs to start again and follow the guidelines at the beginning of the chapter. She asks for the impossible, gives no information about herself, and comes across as angry with men who have done her wrong in the past.

Newly widowed 85-year-old woman, still active as a psychotherapist in White Plains, NY, would like to meet a gentleman of similar age, with a sense of humor and a capacity for closeness.

This is an excellent ad. Succinct and quite clear about what the writer is seeking.

Are you the love of my life? Incurable romantic, 63-years-young divorced woman looking for companionship with a caring, gentle, sensitive man. I live in San Francisco, but am a world traveler. You would be a nonsmoker and not married. I'm voluptuous with a bubbly personality and can make you laugh. Photo appreciated.

Great ad but instead of asking for a man who's "not married," she might ask instead for a man who's single, divorced or widowed.

Set off for my first life's adventure in 1965 to Florida with some friends. I left Florida with a traveling fair which was working its way up to Three Rivers, Quebec. It was fun going from town to town. I worked one of the stands to make spending money. It was the 60s then and normal to drift around and pretend you were free.

Although this ad, from a 68-year-old woman working as a waitress in a Colorado small town, is somewhat rambling, she paints a picture of her past that helps reveal her values and personality.

Beautiful, sexy, spirited widow, dancer/writer, just turned 50, with gentle voice, expressive eyes, seeks smart good man, 55–65, NS, fit, who loves college basketball. For companionship, contentment, write.

What a winner! How could any man resist?

Dark-eyed beauty: at once sophisticated, playful, enchanting. Graceful, trim, curvy. Great-looking. Divorced, NYC professional — artist at heart. Expressive, passionate, adventurous both in mind and spirit. Drawn to travel, sunlight, the outdoors, NPR. Known for wry humor, great sense of fun. Loves Matisse, good wine, walking anywhere, interesting ideas. Seeks divorced/widowed man, 48–63, who smiles easily.

Great illustration of the value of specific details.

A rare treasure. Naturally pretty

girl-next-door with sleek, playful, athletic twist. Long blonde hair, high cheekbones, heart-melting smile. Fine-boned, slim, confident. Patient and passionate. Unafraid to laugh, believes in hopes and dreams. Gentle, honorable, light of heart. Happy anywhere, often prefers outdoors to in: hiking, tennis, running, snowshoeing, sailing. Known for strong aesthetic sense. Never tires of art and music. Vermont resident, drives to Boston at drop of a hat. Loves Southern France, northern Italy, dogs, reading, daisies. Seeks kind, nonsmoking, divorced/widowed man, 49–65.

Another ad with great specific details. Let's hope her photo matches her words.

In how many cities do you imagine making love during retirement? What are your top three? Please explain. SWJF, 57, with high energy, high hopes, and high standards is wondering.

This ad emphasizes sexual adventure and travel but it sounds like that's what the writer wants.

NYC area unattached academic — 61, 5'2", theater/film/lit lover, seeking some drama of my own. Probably not farce, definitely not tragedy. Looking high and low for a kind man with a sense of the absurd.

Indicates a nice sense of humor.

Responding to responses

Acknowledge every communication with a polite reply. Even if you're not interested in additional communication or in meeting with the person, you *must* reply.

If you're not interested, say something like this: "Thank you for contacting me. It's flattering to receive an inquiry but I'm not sure we have much in common. I'd prefer not to pursue this, but I wish you the best in your search."

Don't use phrases that imply you might be in touch in the future or that you may change your mind. Don't leave any doors open for further contact if you've decided you want no more.

Let's hope for the best. You've found someone you'd like to get to know. If you've met on a dating site, you'll usually exchange several e-mails before deciding to meet. Ask questions. The worst that can happen is that your correspondent ignores your questions. The preferred consequence is getting a lot of information in advance. Tell stories. Learn what you have in common. Be real. It's often easier to reveal yourself in writing before a relationship begins.

But these are only the preliminaries. Hearing the sound of someone's voice is the following step. Seeing their eyes is next. It's hard to say at what point to move forward to that chat on the phone or make an in-person date. I think it's a mistake to linger too long in any one stage of communication because you risk getting comfortable and possibly stuck in that phase. If a face-to-face relationship is what you seek, you need to push forward beyond e-mail or chat-only communication. Take the plunge and agree to meet.

⊷ 5 ⊶

More than 50 Ways to Meet Your Lover

The Internet is a great option for meeting and getting to know people. So are phone calls and e-mails. But sooner or later you have to go out of your house. You can't expect to find the love of your life while sitting in front of your TV in your fuzzy slippers.

If you've been feeling lonely, participating in activities where you can meet other people will provide many benefits. You might not meet your true love but you might find some good friends instead. The extra vitality that comes from actively using your mind and your body will make you feel better about yourself and make you more attractive to others.

You don't have to transform yourself into a gregarious party person. Use your natural qualities to facilitate connections.

Even shyness can bring you into contact with others — if you sign up for a class on overcoming shyness. Or simply volunteer for an activity, for instance, as an usher at the symphony, where you'll have a natural opportunity to meet new people.

Think of a new attitude rather than a new personality. While looking for a companion, focus on being open and reaching out to others. Possibilities are all around you. Every place you go might be the place where you'll either meet your mate or meet someone who can introduce you to him or her.

Veronica thought she recognized the gray-haired man in the torn sweater and scruffy jeans in front of her in the line at her local coffee shop. She had recently attended a Christmas party for the company down the hall from her office and wondered if she's met him there. Possibly he was on the janitorial staff in her building. She smiled at him and started a conversation and he invited her to join him at a table. Over their coffees she learned he was the CEO of the company down the hall. He just didn't bother to dress up when he was simply running errands in his own neighborhood.

Practice

Think of every opportunity as a chance to polish your skills in reaching out to others. Practice on the person sitting next to you on the plane, knowing you'll never see them again. Practice on the guy standing behind you in the line at the coffee shop. The more you rehearse, the more natural your efforts will become. You're not likely to find a companion through such casual contacts. But you never know.

Milt, a 68-year-old lawyer from Miami, was in Washington D.C. during the month of December for a convention. Alone and with nothing to do on a Saturday night, he decided to go see a movie. If Leila, a usually shy teacher, hadn't gotten up the nerve to comment on how cold it was while they were waiting in line, they would never have met. Her casual remark led to a longer conversation. They sat together during the movie and discussed it afterwards over dessert. Milt didn't spend any more time in Washington D.C. on his own for Leila was happy to show him around.

General strategies

The odds that the Prince will come knocking on your door with the glass slipper are slim. Even Cinderella had to go out of the house to meet him. You need to be proactive as well. Besides, being active will help you feel like you're in control of your own destiny.

Be realistic. A goal of one activity a week might be reasonable for some and too much for others. You don't have to attend events designed specifically for singles if that makes you uncomfortable. Instead, sign up for activities you enjoy for their own sake; you're likely to meet other people who share your interests but even if you don't, you'll have a good time. Keep in mind that those who move in the same social circles often find romance within that circle. You enhance your chances of finding a date by joining groups.

Don't be afraid to go to events by yourself. Singles appear more approachable than men or women in pairs or groups. You might cringe at the idea of dining alone or going to a movie by yourself. But you're much more likely to be noticed and befriended if alone than if you take along a companion. The same is true for attending any social event, like the opera, a charity auction or a dance.

Don't discount singles' organizations. Collect their newsletters and publications. Tear ads from newspapers or monthly magazines. Get on mailing lists. Ignore requests for donations, but consider attending events. File these invitations away and take them out when you're looking for new places to meet people.

Have a card ready to hand to someone you would like to see again. When the time comes — which it will — you won't have to fish for a pencil and scribble your name on a scrap torn from a napkin. Even if you're not in business, have a simple card printed on nice, heavy stock with your name, phone number, and e-mail. Store the cards in an attractive carrier and keep it handy.

Make it easy for someone to talk to you. When you're out at a coffee shop or restaurant, bring along a book with a snappy title. Or wear a pin or T-shirt proclaiming your political opinions or causes. Carry your laptop, walk a dog, or carry a musical instrument. Such items are likely to get a conversation off the ground.

Talk to everyone you know

In a gentle, but positive way, tell everyone you know — your friends, colleagues,
relatives, doctor, even the receptionist in
the doctor's office — that you're looking:
You might say something like this: "I have
a favor to ask. I'm ready to meet an interesting man (or woman) to go out with.
Would you keep me in mind if you run
into anyone appropriate? I'd be really
grateful." Be sure to tell your single
friends, "If you want, I'll do the same for
you."

Don't apologize for being direct in your
request. Embarrassment projects insecurity and your quest is less likely to be taken
seriously. If you're asked what sort of
person you'd like to meet, keep your answer short. You don't want to eliminate
somebody who might be perfect because
your criteria were too limiting. Say yes
when offered a chance to meet a friend of a
friend, even if the person doesn't sound
like someone you would pick for yourself.

If given an introduction, don't over-
whelm your go-between with questions.
And don't reject someone out of hand because they're "not your type." Try to set
up a meeting that de-emphasizes the

dating aspect of the introduction.

If you were part of a couple, but are now single, don't give up your friendships with couples. You might not be comfortable on some occasions, but you can still socialize with them. Invite a couple or two over to your house for dinner. Make it clear you're not willing to gossip about your ex; instead focus on the interests you have in common. Perhaps your friends will be willing to introduce you to their other single friends. There's the chance your friends will know of another unattached person and will open the door to an introduction.

Staying within your budget

Making a huge investment to meet a companion is a big gamble. Even if you could afford to spend a week at a Swiss ski resort frequented by movie stars, that doesn't guarantee you'll find romance with one.

Suppose you splurge on an activity — say a fancy fund-raiser — so you can socialize with an upper-crust set. It might be fun and maybe you'll meet the wealthy companion of your dreams. On the other hand, you may be setting yourself up for heartache. What do you do after the first date? You won't be able to hide your financial status from a potential mate. And there are risks. Fortune hunters as well as fortunes lurk in expensive places.

Places with promise

Your best chance at success in dating will follow if you simply focus on activities that interest you or your ideal partner.

- For women: go where the men are. Try the boat show, a car show, or a fly fishing demonstration. Wine tastings, at least in my home city of Seattle, often attract more men than women. Join the chamber of commerce if you're in business. Join the finance, not the hospitality, committee of your organization.
- For men: go where the women are. I bet you never thought of trying a quilting class. You'll find all sorts of women just dying to help you thread your needle! You're also likely to be popular if you sign up for a dance class or attend dances, where there are usually more women than men.

- For either gender: Linger when you go out of the house. Have a cup of tea in the café attached to your local plant store. You can start a conversation with someone about what plant to buy or give as a gift. No interest in greenery? Instead of buying your latte to go, sit down and enjoy yourself, watching others. Ride your bicycle when you go to the coffee shop. Wearing athletic gear of any sort is a natural way to start a chat. Or bring along a cute dog, a cute baby, or a topical book or magazine.
- Bookstores provide a perfect opportunity for conversation. Go to a section you like and ask the person browsing there to recommend a title. Be ready to keep the conversation going until it takes on a life of its own. Book-signings are a good bet, since presumably you share an interest in the author. While you're waiting in line to purchase a signed copy of the book, you can strike up a conversation about the author, similar books, and so forth.
- Art galleries and museums are also good. Go on the docent-led tours so you're with a group. Comment to your neighbor on what you're seeing. Hang out in the museum's courtyard or café. Carry a guidebook or a book about the artist

whose work is on exhibit. Talk to the museum guards. They often have advanced degrees in art or are artists trying to make a living. Go to openings. It won't be hard to get on the mailing list. When you've gone to one opening, you'll get invited to others. Conversation is as readily available as the wine and cheese.

- Craft fairs, festivals, and auctions are great places for wandering and meeting people. The phrase, "What do you think of . . ." is a universal opening line.
- Discussion groups. Find them in the paper and on the Internet. Different groups focus on politics, books, health, and food. Sharing opinions is a fine way to connect.
- Sports events provide a perfect opportunity to meet fellow enthusiasts. If you feel you're too old to join a soccer team or run a marathon, volunteer. Volunteers at sporting events usually have the opportunity to chat with both athletes and other volunteers. Give out drinks; monitor the finish line, sign up the riders: talk, smile, and, above all, look interested.
- Join a walking group for a neighborhood tour. Try a garden tour in the spring or a guided walk sponsored by a neighborhood historical society. An unattached

tourist might be delighted to talk to a resident.

- Hiking. Try day trips such as a hike at a comfortable level of difficulty. You want to enjoy what you see and have enough breath to talk to the people around you.
- The public library. Today libraries have more than books. You'll find concerts, discussion groups, lectures, and computer classes. Many libraries have activities specifically for those over 50.
- Religious connections. Most churches have singles' groups. If your local church doesn't, you can probably find another one nearby that does. Even if you don't have a religious preference, you may enjoy participating in singles' events at a church with beliefs compatible with yours.
- Parents Without Partners is not just for people who have young children. Some members joined when their children were young but years later, still rely on this organization as a source of social activities.
- Clubs. Don't be intimidated by clubs with names such as the "Yacht Club" or "Mountaineers." You don't need a boat or an interest in climbing Everest to join.

148

These are often loose-knit organizations with a focus on social activities as well as sports. No experience is needed to sign up for beginner's classes in tennis or golf. Outward Bound has a senior program — an ideal way of acquiring survival and team skills. Don't overlook clubs for game devotees, such as bridge, chess, and Scrabble.

- Fund-raisers and ethnic activities. Watch for ethnic activities such as the Swedish pancake breakfast or the fire department charity barbecue. There are big tables for people who go alone and want to sit with others.

- Lectures. Attending a lecture, or better still, a series of talks, provides a great topic for conversation. If you attend more than one lecture in a series, you have a better chance of getting to know people. Find a schedule in your newspaper or local university and attend, even if the subject is only mildly interesting. Choose prestigious locations or places that smack of elegance. The audience is likely to be filled with sophisticated, educated listeners. Then it's up to you to turn to the person sitting beside you and ask a question or make a comment that starts a conversation.

Finding Classes

How do you find classes? The Internet is your greatest source of information. I strongly recommend becoming familiar with this super resource. If you are one of those reluctant to join the computer age, ask your librarian to help.

How to access your information on the Net? You'll need to be willing to try different combinations of words but a fine place to start is by typing "seniors classes" in the bar on Google or your favorite search engine. When I tried I got 647,000 results (really). These included tips for the high school senior prom so you'll need to narrow your search. You might also want to add your city such as "senior classes Albuquerque." Look at the treasure I found:

Continuing education program sponsored by Eastern Michigan University for people over 50 in southeastern Michigan. Offers variety of classes and workshops. Member-shaped organization with peer teachers; no tests, exams, or grades. Most classes meet at the Senior Health Building. Annual dues $20. Class fees $5–$25 (reduced for members). An e-mail contact address is provided.

And, at the same time I found this, look what else appeared in the same search as the classes in eastern Michigan. Hard to tell if this activity is for people in your age range but the only way to find out is to contact them and ask.

"SPICE of Life" Jewish Community Center programs for adults are social, physical, intellectual, cultural and educational. Weekly programming includes Exercise class, Creative Writing Group; quilting and Mah-jongg groups; guest presentations and entertainment, current events discussion and literary groups; and Fri. Yiddish groups. "Seniors on Stage" is a reader's theater troupe. Also provides opportunities for meeting newcomers to the community, participating in intergenerational programs, and volunteer activities. The Matinee Musicale series features members of the Ann Arbor Symphony Orchestra.

These are only two examples of thousands and thousands of possibilities.

Permit me to remind you that you, too, have countless opportunities. Use your imagination, take heart and find your love!

- Classes. Adult education is big business and many classes are filled with middle-aged singles. Find courses at the community college, the YMCA, the university's continuing education department, the park department and community centers. Suppose you have an interest but think only younger people will be in your class? So what! When you have a mutual interest, people soon forget your age. Try seminars that fill your needs of the moment, such as stress management, interpersonal skills, personal finance, self-image improvement or a divorce-adjustment seminar. Take the largest class you can find because you'll have the greatest number of people to meet. It doesn't matter if you sit next to someone younger, older, or of the same gender. If you connect with anyone in the class, you'll look animated and approachable. Many courses are gender neutral, like cooking, investments, ceramics, jewelry-making, chess, or bridge. You might not meet the love of your life but you might learn to make a killer quiche and make friends with someone with a single cousin who's just right for you.
- Classes popular with women. Yoga and aerobics classes often attract a dispropor-

tionate number of women, providing an ideal opportunity for men. A pudgy body is — really and truly — something women will overlook. In such a setting, women will speak with you and offer encouragement. Like all other activities, you need to show up on several occasions so that your face is familiar. You don't need to justify your choice. Just select a subject that piques your interest, for instance, needleworking, knitting or crochet. When a small group of New England men got together to make a quilt for a charity project, they had such a good time that they kept on meeting. They call themselves "Men of the Cloth," and often display their work at quilt shows, which are usually filled with women. Before becoming a psychiatrist, I was a surgeon. I spent a lot of time in the operating room lounge with its predominance of male surgeons. Some did needlepoint or crocheted. They were used to doing fine work with their hands and liked keeping busy between cases. Men have a very good chance of having the pick of the classroom if they sign up for a course filled with females. Women will admire you for your courage as well as your vulnerability.

- Classes popular with men. Women can take subjects that are traditionally thought of as men's domain. Carpentry, auto mechanics, beer-making and fly-fishing courses are usually full of men. Or pick something you would have never dreamed of doing such as bicycle repair or welding. Why not?
- Dance classes. You don't need a partner to study dance. Explore the many types of dancing available in your community. Some are more likely to attract older people than others, but you will find seniors at the lindy dances and young-sters learning tango.
- Teaching a class. Teaching is a great way to meet people who are interested in the same things that interest you. Even if you've never taught before, think about your life experience and what you might share with others. Community centers, adult education centers, and local sin-gles' groups welcome people who can teach a one-day class or a series of short workshops on subjects such as cooking, starting a business, retirement planning or how to manage sadness. If you're in the health profession, use your back-ground to teach about nutrition, how to avoid a heart attack, or any of hundreds

of subjects. There's usually little pay, but you benefit by meeting others. I used to teach a watercolor course, the sort of art class predominantly taken by women. The men who did sign up always got lots of attention from their female classmates.

- Expand your horizons. Try attending a science fiction group, a seminar on Italian films, a short course on making cheese. Who knows who you'll meet.

Travel

Maybe you've been dreaming about spending your retirement years exploring exotic places and visiting the world's great cities with your sweetheart. No, you don't have to find your darling before you set off on your adventure. You may find that special person while you're out and about.

Cruises

Certain cruises and cruise lines will serve your needs better than others. Here's the rule of thumb: *Longer-colder-older.* Translated: the longer the itinerary, the colder the destination, the older the cruise passengers. Cost also plays a major role, but try rhyming that.

If you're trying to avoid the junior set:

- Be wary of the flashy "fun! fun! fun!" cruise lines like Carnival and Disney, which cater to a young crowd and families with small children.
- On cruise lines like Holland America and Celebrity, even in the Caribbean, you'll find fewer people under the age of 25.
- With destinations like Alaska and Northern Europe, the number of younger passengers is significantly smaller.
- On the most upscale lines, such as Radisson and Seven Seas, the average clientele is over 55 and affluent.

You'll want to investigate this option with great care before committing to ten days or so at sea. Does your cruise line offer special senior prices on selected sailings? Carnival has a senior discount program for members of the American Association of Retired Persons.

Cruises offer many travel adventures — you can discover ancient ruins, explore jungles, gaze at scenic vistas, or simply enjoy living in a luxurious floating resort. Use the web to find a cruise to suit your wishes. Think about your budget and the length of time you want to spend. A good site is: seniorssearch.com, then select the "travel" option and see the nifty possibilities.

Educational vacations

Look into a volunteer vacation. If you spend two weeks rebuilding a Mexican school shattered by an earthquake, you're going to meet some good-hearted people.

Organizations such as the Smithsonian Institution sponsor elegant trips for various age and interest groups. You can learn about art, astronomy or history in the United States or abroad on trips guided by museum or university experts. Often these offerings attract well-educated and sophisticated travelers. Pricey, but you definitely get what you pay for.

Check out the offerings of universities, museums, and language schools. You might find a trip within your means that offers an educational as well as social experience.

Elderhostel: If you're 55 or older, this organization offers a marvelous array of educational opportunities around the world.

You can trace the footsteps of Lewis & Clark, get an insider's view of the Louvre, wander the battlefields of Gettysburg, study Shakespeare, Dickinson, or Frost, unlock the mysteries of the Dead Sea Scrolls, or set up your easel next to a waterfall. The programs attract 200,000 participants each year. Try: elderhostel.org/welcome/home.asp

Shawguides: This website helps you find educational and travel opportunities tailored to suit your schedule and your interests. For instance, if you type the words "February," "Italy" and "writing class" into the search engine, you'll get a list of writing classes offered in Italy in February. Go to: shawguides.com

Recreation

If your idea of a vacation involves physical and social activities, you can plan your trip around opportunities to snorkel, play tennis or just lay in the sun.

Club Med. This vacation company offers special programs for clients 55 and older to encourage them to participate in getaways where they'll meet others in the same age group.

Sports. Look for vacation packages designed for seniors. If you have access to the Internet, type terms like "seniors" and the name of your favorite sport into a search engine. That's how I found this web site designed to offer skiing opportunities for those over 50: skicentral.com/seniors.html

Dining out

Don't be shy about going out to eat alone. Choose a restaurant that attracts regulars. It should be busy enough so you'll be able to talk to the person at the next table and quiet enough so they can hear you. Or take a seat at the bar where you can order dinner and you'll be sitting right next to your fellow diner. Ask to borrow a section of the newspaper. Or ask for a recommendation of a dessert. Comment on the rain or the sun. Comment on anything and accompany your remark with a smile. Speak to whoever looks friendly and don't discriminate based on age or gender.

Select a fancy hotel coffee shop or lounge. A complete breakfast may be too expensive, so get a roll and coffee. Linger. Read what others there are reading — you can never tell what you might find in the *New York Times*. Dress like others. Keep returning to the same place. It's a great opening for someone else if they note you're a regular.

Pets and plants

These are two great modes for meeting others. Dog walking is an old standby. If you don't have a dog, borrow your friend's or, better still, get a dog in your life. (A dog is much more reliable than most human companions, not to mention more loyal, loving, and furrier. Sigh. But this is a book about meeting humans.)

Get a pet that conveys your personal message. Pit bulls and itty-bitty terriers say one thing. Nice, middle sized, smart, clean poodles indicate something else about their owner. Be sure your dog has good manners — you don't want your pooch planting muddy paws on that special someone's chest.

Gardening is another great way to meet others. To get yourself out of your own yard, sign up for classes, workshops, and greenhouse tours. If you have a specialty, like orchids, dahlias or native plants, find and join an association for others with the same interest. If your city has community gardens, reserve a plot. You'll get to know your fellow horticulturists at work parties, organized social events, and while working side-by-side on sunny days; you'll also meet the visitors that wander through the garden to admire it.

Volunteer

Volunteer opportunities are extensive and having a common interest gives you something to discuss. Try public radio or television fund-raisers or walks to raise money for research. You can talk with people walking along with you and at the closing ceremonies when everyone feels open and approachable. What to talk about? Ask if the person next to you is wearing comfortable shoes.

Volunteer to usher at a theater or concert hall. You not only get to see wonderful performances, but you'll meet and greet members of the audience. Volunteer to work at your community theater even if you have no ambitions to perform. You can help with scenery, costumes, or tickets. A production bonds the participants in a special way.

If you have a religious affiliation, volunteer to help with services, community outreach, or food preparation. You can attend services for your own spiritual enlightenment, but there's nothing better than a social group for meeting new people.

Join the friends of the library group or the group that cleans up trash along the riverbank or plants trees to make the community green.

Volunteer for a political campaign. You'll meet all sorts of people who share your beliefs whether it's for a candidate or for a cause. Since you're working for free, you can be choosy about your assignment. If you're asked to file papers in the back room, say no. Your time is better served if you're working with others.

Volunteer at the hospital. Choose the gift shop because you'll have more opportunity to meet visitors and employees rather than the patients.

Support groups

If you're coping with a problem such as cancer, caring for aging parents, chemical dependency, divorce, or bereavement you have a good reason to seek a support group. People in these groups are often at different stages. They may need more time than you do to cope with an illness or loss and may not be ready for a new relationship. Stay in touch after the group has ended. Six months later your friendship may blossom into romance.

Organizations

Service organizations, such as Rotary Club or your chamber of commerce, are a great way to get acquainted with new people. Call and ask if you can sit in on a meeting. Begin a conversation with the person sitting next to you by asking what he or she does. If the meeting is interesting, ask if you can come again.

Serve on boards. Find a cause that interests you. Consider nonprofit organizations like a crisis clinic or a shelter for the homeless or abused. Inquire about organizations that provide funds for artists, preserve history, or advise small businesses. Boards are a great way to meet employed, involved people.

Involvement in the arts offers wonderful opportunities. Call the offices of the opera, the museum, or the ballet. Ask to train as a docent. Inquire about classes or ongoing groups you can attend. Perhaps you can volunteer in the ticket office or backstage.

Do you identify with a particular ethnic heritage? Call the Museum of African American Art or the Scandinavian Cultural Center. Discussing your mutual heritage will give you an instant bond with other members. These organizations usually sponsor outings, dinners, and craft shows. Some offer language classes, movies, and travel opportunities.

How about an ethnic heritage you've always found intriguing? Maybe you're Italian but you've always been curious about Norwegians. Find the Sons of Norway in the phone book. Attend a lecture on the Vikings. Talk to the person next to you. "Is your family from Norway?" People are always happy to help you learn about the things that interest them. Ask for a recommendation for language classes and books. Although you might be more comfortable if you go someplace where you fit in, you may get more attention if you're the "different" one.

Shopping

Plenty of people tell stories about how they met at the supermarket checkout line. This might be a long shot but well worth a try. You might get a pleasant but brief reply when you ask for a recommendation on a wine or comment on the items in someone's shopping basket, but you might also begin a conversation. I have a woman friend who sometimes spends her Saturday afternoons trolling the men's department, looking for men she can ask for advice about buying her brother a birthday gift. Of course, unless you really like shopping, I think you'd be better off spending your time in activities where you have repeated exposure to the same people and a common interest to focus your conversation.

Blind dates

From time to time, your well-meaning friends might invite you over to meet someone they think is special or set you up on a blind date. Always remember to call and thank your friends no matter how awful the evening was. Say something like: "Thanks so much for trying. It was really interesting meeting Charlie although it wasn't a match. Please keep me in mind for next time."

Marie was recovering from a broken heart when her coworker, Nicole, suggested she should meet Frank, Nicole's neighbor, whose wife had died two years earlier. Marie wanted to date politically liberal men who were taller than her six feet. Frank was not only shorter (at five feet, eight inches) but he was a confirmed

> "Service organizations, such as Rotary Club or your chamber of commerce, are a great way to get acquainted with new people."

Republican. Frank wanted to meet a short, Catholic woman like his late wife. Marie resisted Nicole's attempts to introduce her to Frank for several months but finally gave in. To her surprise, she and Frank found genuine pleasure in each other's company.

Singles' clubs

Many people avoid joining singles' clubs because they don't like being so obvious about their search for a date. But where else can you socialize with a room full of other single adults? You'll be more inclined to attend the club's activities if you already have friends in the group. The more functions you attend, the greater the opportunity to make friends. There's usually a constant influx of new faces, giving you the chance to view even more potential matches.

Every city has several singles' clubs. Don't just bounce around from club to club but visit one several times. Get to know people by interacting with them at holidays and attending events. It may take a while before you know if these are people whose company you enjoy. Think of it in these terms: You're seeing if you like them, not waiting to be chosen.

Some singles' clubs, such as "Single Booklovers," are not clubs, but dating schemes which connect people based on interests in books. This isn't necessarily bad. Just be aware of what you're signing up for when you join the club.

Matchmakers

My experience and those of my friends with individual matchmakers has been disappointing. I've responded to a few ads for matchmaking services. The prices were extremely high and the services limited. I recommend you focus your efforts elsewhere.

Dating services

In your search for a companion you will be spending either your time or your money. If you use a dating service, you'll be spending your money rather than your time. Make sure you spend it wisely. These services often cost thousands and there's no assurance you'll get value for what you pay.

There are many types of dating services. I responded to an ad placed by a company which operated out of a storefront in an office park. A young person who looked like she had just graduated from high school asked me to fill out a form, then took me into a cubicle for a "personal interview," which consisted of a number of silly and irrelevant questions. The longer the interview went on, the more suspicious I became. Finally the youngster departed, supposedly to make copies, and an older employee moved in for the kill: getting my signature on a contract that required large monthly payments.

This is a grim scenario, but not the only one. Reputable dating services do exist and you can track their records by asking for references which, in my opinion, may not be entirely useful. You will be given only the names of satisfied clients — you're not going to hear the horror stories.

Call the Better Business Bureau to learn if there have been complaints registered or if the service is legitimate.

Safeguard yourself by preparing a list of questions whose answers must satisfy:

- Will the person who interviews you be the person who matches you?
- What success has this company had with older people?
- What are the details of the contract? What happens if they are unable to match you? What happens if your matches are inappropriate?
- How are clients screened?
- What percent of active members are in your age range?
- What types of memberships are offered? Short term or long term?

Don't be fooled if the interviewer says they have just the right person in mind for you. This is a typical answer designed to get you to sign instantly. Take your time and don't be seduced by this lure.

Some dating services offer personality testing so they can offer appropriate matches. Others let members review the profiles and choose. Some use videos or picture albums of clients. See which, if any, feels comfortable for you.

Before signing a contract, be specific about how many introductions you will receive and the criteria which must be met for you to be satisfied. If you agree to take a personality profile test, ask to see your scores and those of the person considered a match. Ask what kind of compensation the service will provide for mismatches. If the service has been in business for years and can boast a reasonable track record, signing for a reasonable length of time at a comfortable price might be worth the effort.

Exercise

Maybe you think you'll scream if one more person tells you to join a health club. Don't worry. I do think joining a health club is a great idea. But I don't think it's a good way to find a date. It might work if you look spiffy in spandex, but many older men and women are too self-conscious to offer their aging bodies for that sort of scrutiny.

If you want to meet someone through the medium of exercise, choose something where you can stay comfortably clothed. Golf is a sport that attracts men and women of all ages and at every level from beginner to pro. Take a class with other people at your level. You'll meet enthusiasts you can talk to, practice with, and play with for years to come. If golf isn't your thing, look for a walking group or a back-to-bicycling group. Think about which sport you've always wanted to try and sign up for lessons.

Some older adults who have persistent medical conditions may not consider exercise an option, but new evidence suggests otherwise. Researchers studied a group of adults aged 65 to 87 who had chronic illnesses, and found those who adhered to a prescribed exercise regimen had greater long-term survival compared with similar patients who did not. Get your doctor's go-ahead, and then begin your activity.

If you haven't participated in group exercise since high school gym class, you may want to try yoga, aqua aerobics, or weight training classes. An Australian study published in *Preventive Medicine* shows that women who trained with a group were better able than solo exercisers to stick to a regular fitness routine. And not surprisingly, the women who were instructed to exercise at a moderate level were more successful at following their exercise routines than those who were expected to exercise vigorously. Group classes offer social and moral support; group camaraderie keeps individual members motivated. In addition, it's easier for fitness professionals to individualize an exercise routine and monitor progress when the participants are attending a class, and it is also easier for exercisers to get immediate feedback on their progress.

Not sure where to sign up for exercise classes? Many senior centers and Y's offer programs. You can also check with your health care provider and the local hospital to see what is available.

Singles newsletters

Try entering this term in your computer's search engine and you'll find a wealth of possibilities. Refine your search and add qualifying terms such as "ivy league" or "divorced" and your possibilities expand! I found "The Ivy League 50-Plus Singles, established by the Yale Club of Washington, D.C." in my first search using Google!

The most unlikely places

At age 63, my friend Robbie had given up on finding a wife. He works in the computer field, is slim, fit and smart and a truly caring person. Yet ever since adolescence he has been seeking the right woman with no success. Even years of therapy haven't helped him figure out what prevented him from forming lasting attachments. As a long-term member of a writing group, he was frequently fixed up with dates by his fellow writers. He also attended singles' clubs, took ballroom dancing classes, and both answered and placed personals ads. But nothing worked.

Then last year he started talking to the woman sitting next to him in the waiting room at his doctor's. He had gone for a routine checkup but she was there for an oncology referral. Roxanne was the same age as Robbie and he could tell by looking at her that she was seriously ill. She was gaunt and pale, her eyes were sunken and she was having trouble breathing. Robbie waited until her appointment was over, helped her into her car, and offered to assist her with grocery shopping the next day. Her boyfriend had disappeared as it became obvious that Roxanne was sick. In fact, he might react this way, likely was one of the reasons she had put off seeking medical attention.

A romance flourished between Robbie and Roxanne. They both knew she was dying but they still had the most romantic and caring six months imaginable. Rob didn't regret a moment of their time together. He felt this brief relationship was one of the best experiences of his lifetime because he had really found love.

Some words of advice

When you meet someone for the first time, there's a fairly good chance that both of you are anxious. You may be troubled by shyness, aging, or your respective pasts. So don't place too much importance on that first encounter. A diamond in the rough can look pretty dull at first sight. Likewise, you might meet someone who seems way out of your league. Keep in mind people may be quite different than they first appear. Unless you get clear evidence of incompatibility, give the person a second chance.

The woman sitting next to you at the art lecture may be too shy to talk. Even a normally friendly person might be preoccupied with a problem or feeling withdrawn because of a recent rejection. Keep trying. If you're sociable, but not intrusive, if you keep looking for common ground, you may awaken their interest.

Sometimes it's the other way around and you're being chatted up by someone who's trying too hard. Cut them some slack. They may be so nervous about connecting with you that their anxiety makes them clumsy.

At times it seems like people aren't trying at all. You start a conversation and the other person keeps mentioning her former boyfriend. Maybe she comments on how much she loves men with thick, curly hair while you cringe, aware of your unmistakable state of baldness. Or you introduce yourself and the person gets your name wrong twice. Just remember how many times in the past you made a mistake and wished you had been given a second chance.

Don't reject someone just because they don't seem to meet your dream wishes. They may not be tall enough, shapely enough, young enough. They may not enjoy your favorite sport or activity. Wishes are preference. Needs are essential.

Establish your credibility early. Offer your full name. This indicates you don't want to hide it and will encourage the other person to state his, if he's so inclined. If he doesn't, that tells you something.

Let the other person know you're single without broadcasting this as an undesirable state. You want them to know you're available if they should choose to follow up the lead you're offering. Mention you're looking forward to the next theater excursion with your singles' group. Talk about how you prefer eating out because you don't like cooking for one. Say you're looking for a partner for bridge or chess. Comment on some nice family activity or something else that makes you appear normal, for instance, taking your nephew to a baseball game or attending church services. Don't wear any ring on the fourth finger of your left hand. Get the picture? The message you want to send is that you're single, safe and sane.

⋘ 6 ⋙

First Date

Here you are. It's your first date and you're electrified by mutual attraction. You really connect. You planned to meet for thirty minutes, but seven hours later you're still talking and have plenty more to say. You recognize how much you have in common. Your mutual understanding is instant and complete. This is the peak moment of a lifetime. It's hard to leave, but you know you'll be meeting again soon. Your lives will be intertwined from this point forward. . . .

Nice fantasy! But this scenario doesn't remotely resemble reality.

Sure, there's a chance it could happen like this. But it's more likely you'll be angst-ridden before the date and disappointed afterwards.

If you enjoyed dating when you were younger, you might enjoy it now. But for many people dating is an anxious and awkward experience, fraught with opportunities for rejection. It's even worse if you're pinning your hopes on this particular person, praying you'll meet your true love so you won't have to go on another date with a stranger.

Be reassured. Your date is probably harboring the same fears and dreams.

Assume you'll do your best. In spite of your good intentions, you might make mistakes. It's too bad, but it can't be helped. Everyone makes mistakes when they are learning a new behavior. You'll have plenty of future chances for improvement.

Think of this date as a first step. Dating is a process and it takes time. Sure, you'd like to find instant chemistry, mutual attraction, and common interests. That's the ideal. But there are many other possible outcomes. If you approach the situation with curiosity rather than rigid expectations, you'll be less likely to be disappointed.

Remember, the important issue is whether you like your date, rather than the other way around. Making the other person like you is beyond your control. Keeping this in mind will help you relax.

Setting the scene

Reduce the fantasy factor. Consider yourself fortunate if you've previously met your date on neutral ground. You've seen her eyes and movements, observed her smile, and sensed her interest. You know you'd like to get to know her better.

When meeting someone you've found through a personal ad, you have fewer cues. It is to your benefit to gather advance information. Set the date up by telephone so you can hear the person's voice. Ask for a snapshot so you will recognize him.

Cindy thought she and Bob had a good connection over the phone. They talked for over twenty minutes. But when they agreed to meet, Bob started asking for specifics about her appearance. When she said she was "five foot one," there was a long silence. Then he told her he didn't date women under five seven and hung up. Although Cindy was disappointed, she was also relieved. "It was better to be rejected sight unseen. If we had gotten together and he didn't want to see me again, I would have assumed he didn't like something I said or the way I looked. My height is just a fact. I can't grow six inches."

Set time limits and specify your preference for place. "How about if we meet for a half hour at (name of place)? Would 7:30 on Thursday be all right for you?" This precludes expectations of a longer or more elaborate date. You don't need to make an advance excuse such as, "I'm expecting my cousin from Omaha at nine and I have to be home to get ready." That might make it seem like you're squeezing your date in between other activities. Just specify your preference; no need to qualify or explain.

An open-ended date may lock you into an uncomfortable situation. Even if you like each other, a first date lasting seven hours is unwise. You need time to absorb what has just happened. You may feel differently about your experience after a few days of consideration. Understand the only purpose of the first date is to find out if you want a second one. You don't have to decide whether or not you want to get married.

A half hour is a comfortable length of time to spend with a person you've never met before. It gives you the chance to accomplish what you set out to do: see the person face to face, get a sense of how the person talks, walks, and looks. Are there barriers impossible to overcome? Is there a discomforting height discrepancy? Does

181

your date look far younger or older than you expected? Does her parole officer feature prominently in the conversation?

> *"Set time limits and specify your preference for place. 'How about if we meet for a half hour at [name of place]? Would 7:30 on Thursday be all right for you?' This precludes expectations of a longer or more elaborate date."*

Get together when most people socialize. Some times are better than others. Select a weekend, workday evening, or after-dinner hour. Odd hours like six in the morning or eleven at night suggest you're too busy or preoccupied to make room in your life for another person. Don't ask for a coffee date with a new person on Christmas Eve or any holiday. Looking desperate is terribly unattractive.

Confirm the date. If you've set up your date in advance, call or e-mail the day before to confirm. If you hear, "I'm really looking forward to meeting you. But I need to tell you I just reconnected with my high school sweetheart and I'm flying out to meet him next week," you might want to cancel. Or at least postpone until after the reunion.

Avoid a date you sense is pitting you against the competition. Don't try to raise your endorphins by edging out some unseen man or woman. Run a marathon if you're seeking a competitive high. It's nearly impossible to compete with a new love interest. Why start when odds are low? As hard as it may be, I don't recommend meeting with someone who tells you he has just met a fabulous woman, perhaps in response to the same ad you answered. Instead say: "This doesn't seem like the best time for us to meet. I wish you well with your new interest. Maybe if things don't work out and I'm still available, we could try another time."

Janelle was disappointed when her coffee date, a good-looking stockbroker, kept checking his watch every five minutes. Although he was clearly distracted, she managed to engage him in conversation enough to learn they had similar values and interests so she suggested meeting again. That's when he told her he was in the throes of a new romance and had only met with her because he felt obligated to do so.

Don't force a meeting if it doesn't seem right. You've had your phone conversation and are ready to set the time and place. Then you're bombarded with a rapid pop quiz and feel like you've answered everything wrong. Or maybe you're the one asking the questions and you don't like some of the answers. Don't assume you have to go through with the date just because you've already made plans. Courtesy is a bad reason for meeting. Let it go. It's difficult enough to make a connection when everything is right. You're fighting against poor odds if you try to force something that isn't there.

If you decide to cancel, give notice as soon as possible. Suppose you feel like you just can't go on this date even though you had the best of intentions when you made it. You really have a headache. You've received bad news. You've had a coffee date with the woman of your dreams and want to look no further. What should you do? Honesty is advised, brutal honesty is not. Call as soon as you've made your decision to cancel. Do you want to cancel permanently or do you want to reschedule? That part of the message should be clear. State your reason for canceling. Don't lie. Lies, no matter how small, are transparent and will haunt you later. You don't need to go into detail to make your point. "I have an upset stomach and the diarrhea is just awful," is excessive when "I'm not feeling well," will do nicely. If you want to cancel permanently, you don't need an auxiliary excuse. You might be feeling ill but that's not why you're canceling. Just say something like: "I've been thinking about our conversations and I just don't think we're going to be a match." Always finish delivering the news with your good wishes for the person's future. It's civilized.

Determine how you will identify the other person. As you make your plans to meet, don't ask, "What do you look like?" It puts your companion on the spot. If you're asked, be ready with a response such as "I'm fairly short and I always carry a blue purse." Don't say, "I'm kind of overweight" or other self-disparaging descriptors. Pick your best feature. Or you can avoid the issues of looks by saying something like: "I'll be wearing a brown coat. How will I recognize you?"

Approach the dating process like a job interview. You wouldn't say to a prospective employer, "Oh, I just love your job. I don't need to go home to think about it. I'm going to stay here right now and start work." You'd go home and think about it, call your friends, and think some more. You'd want some time to savor the good fortune of finding something that feels right for you. Your first date is the same. You want to be able to let things sink in.

First Date Advice

- Keep your eyes on your date. Don't convey lack of interest with straying glances.
- Don't fidget. Sit straight. Send a body language message that you're alert and interested.
- Call your date by name.
- Don't tell jokes that can unknowingly offend.
- Don't mention money that you have or wish you had.
- Don't list what's in your collection: art, stamps, cats.
- Compliment but don't overdo. Don't patronize.
- Don't promise to help with something in the future if you're not sure there will be one.
- Don't assume your date's preference for how she'd like her coffee or food. Everyone places his or her own order on that first date.
- If your date has a piece of food on her face, don't reach across to wipe it off and risk getting your hand slapped. Just forget it. It's not going to take root and grow. No need to embarrass anyone,

least of all your potential life partner.
- Don't arrive hungry. Assume you'll have only a coffee and eat enough before so your thoughts will center on your date and not on food.
- Don't exaggerate. You may have to back up your claims in the future. Anyway, you may be carried away in the moment but take a psychiatrist's word: lies are transparent.
- Don't show family snapshots, pictures of when you were fifty pounds lighter or whip out your driver's license to show how you looked ten years ago.
- Don't curse!
- Turn off your cell phone.

My friend, Bella, thought Uri was a dream. He answered her ad in *The Boston Monthly* and they met for coffee at 4 o'clock in Harvard Square. He was a tall, broad-shouldered Israeli who had been in the US for a dozen years. With his patched sweater and his gray beard, he looked like a scholar and his baritone voice and his accent made her shiver. They had so much to talk about that the coffee date turned into a walk, and then dinner at a little Israeli restaurant where they dined on kabobs, falafel and wine. Seven hours later, Uri drove her home. He pointed out his apartment building as they passed it and she could just picture his living room, full of books, and the two of them lounging on the sofa reading the newspaper together on a Sunday afternoon. When he kissed her good night at her door, she was ready to marry him.

He asked for her phone number so he could arrange the next date. "Maybe I should call you," she joked. They had spent a lot of time talking about how men and women are considered equals in Israel and she wanted to let him know she had the same values. She was surprised when he said, "That wouldn't be a good idea." It turned out he lived with a girlfriend who was violently jealous (undoubtedly with good reason). Uri claimed they were breaking up and she just hadn't moved out yet. But Bella had heard enough. The fantasy first date had been just a fantasy.

Choosing the setting

Meet your date in a place that allows you to give full attention to your companion. You don't want a setting resembling a police interrogation room nor do you want someplace overly familiar. If possible, pay an advance visit to the spot. Does it feel comfortable, neutral, and pleasant? How about parking? Will the walk to your car be as brief as possible when you leave? Chain coffeehouses are predictable if not exciting. Since they're a popular setting for people of all ages, you won't feel conspicuous. Your local café where everyone greets you by name and interrupts with questions about your activities is unfair to your date. Avoid distractions and surprises. Meeting your date may be surprise enough.

After two long phone conversations, I agreed to meet Malcolm for coffee at a local popular coffee shop at 10 a.m. on Sunday Morning. He was a 54-year old real estate broker who had been divorced for three years, was doing well in his business and liked opera. I described myself so he could recognize me; he told me he was tall (5'11") and would be wearing a cap. When I walked into the coffee shop, I saw several tall men, some wearing caps, but none looked like they could be my date. I purchased my latte and was sitting down, keeping an eye on people entering the restaurant, when a man who looked like a cross between a homeless person and a criminal on the run, approached me. "Hi," he announced. "I bet you're looking for me. I'm Malcolm." He plopped down in a nearby chair and asked if I'd buy him a decaf. "I like extra sugar," he added. As I had no intention of doing anything except leaving, I declined this request. As I got up to leave, I saw my boss, who was also having his Sunday morning coffee, watching me from across the coffee shop with great amusement.

> *"Lies, no matter how small, are transparent and will haunt you later."*

Do your homework. Visit the place ahead of time. You don't want to learn the coffee shop is about to close as you enter or be turned away from the restaurant because you're not wearing a tie. You risk having to shout by selecting a crowded, child-friendly restaurant on a Saturday afternoon.

The setting should be quiet and respectful of yourself and your date. Remember this is as hard for your date as it is for you. Make it as easy as possible and don't let the environment get in the way.

Mandy was introduced to Ethan by a dating service and they had several promising phone conversations before they decided to meet in person. They agreed to meet in the lobby of Mandy's apartment building and go to a nearby coffee shop to talk. It was winter in Boston and a blizzard was in progress on the day of their date. Still Ethan managed to make it to Mandy's apartment building but he didn't want to go out again into the snow. "Let's get this over with right here," he said. In retrospect, Mandy realizes she should have cancelled the date right then. Instead she spent an hour sitting in the lobby with him, while Ethan peppered her with questions. She was embarrassed by his cold manner during the interrogation, especially since it took place in front of her doorman and her neighbors who were coming home from work. To make matters worse, Ethan left saying he'd call but never did.

Choose a setting that is background and not the focus of the meeting. You should be able to face each other and talk and be able to make an easy exit when ready. If you know of a comfortable place, offer it as a suggestion. For a more chic option than a chain coffeehouse, consider meeting in a museum café. Don't worry about a museum admission fee, as you can usually enter without payment. Try the coffee

Words of Caution

- If you don't know your companion well, don't commit to an extended evening. Hold off on a concert or a movie date with a meal to follow. This could prove a long and painful experience with a person you don't know. Suppose you hate the play and want to leave? Suppose you're bored and doze during the performance? Suppose your companion has breath as bad as a rhinoceros? You'll want the date to end and not have to face an additional hour waiting for dessert to arrive.
- Don't choose an activity where physical exertion is the focus. You may wrongly estimate the fitness level of your companion. Going for a hike might mean walking through a park and admiring the flowers to some people while another person might expect to hike to an elevation of 6,000 feet carrying a fifty-pound pack.
- Avoid competitive activity. Don't suggest a tennis match, chess game, or ping-pong tournament, even if there is a delightful clubhouse coffee shop in which you can unwind after the game. You

don't want to get started on a competitive note.
- Don't go to a party where your date knows no one. Forget first dates at weddings, Valentine's Day, and New Year's Eve.
- No walks with pets or other people. Eliminate distractions even if your date says it's okay to bring along your hundred pound Rottweiler. Your date needs your undivided attention.
- Don't ask your date to your retirement dinner even if you're getting every award under the sun. Ask your niece instead.
- Your living room is too familiar a setting for your first meeting.
- Don't meet at a place where you'll be ill at ease. Pass on a bar if you're a nondrinker. If the buffet restaurant with the super senior specials is not your style, decline even if you qualify for the half-price meat loaf. If you're uneasy with the prospect of dressing up for a first meeting in a posh four-star hotel lounge, suggest an alternative.
- Don't ask your date to the community center's social hour. Meeting a new person for the first time is for twenty to thirty minutes only. You don't want to be distracted by socializing with a crowd.

shop or lounge of an elegant hotel or meet for coffee and dessert in an upscale restaurant. The setting is likely to be quiet and the service unobtrusive.

Make sure the locale is special, but not too cute. The hot dog stand on the corner of Madison and Thirty-Fifth Street might be fine for some, but awkward for most. Even if you love the coffee at the local truck stop; that might not be so delightful for your executive date.

Walks can be nice. First meet to buy your coffees. Arrange the route so it's neither too long nor too physically demanding. Let your date know the plan in advance; some people not be able to walk a long distance, or might find it difficult to walk and talk at the same time. You might also consider the zoo, a sculpture garden, a botanical garden, or a river walk.

Avoid traveling any distance for the first meeting. Rather than drive two hours for a twenty minute get-together, have several advance phone conversations to make sure this is someone in whom you're willing to invest time and energy. Even if you have high hopes, don't make an excessive investment. Suggest a coffee shop close to where you live. If your date finds the place inconvenient, choose a location halfway in between.

It may be old-fashioned, but for a first date, the man should drive the longer distance. Gallantry isn't completely dead.

Dating should be an activity of equals based on mutual interest, so check out specialized activities with your date. If you've previously met, dinner or an activity of mutual interest is a natural plan. Don't simply agree to an activity to make a good impression. For instance, don't agree to go sailing if you hate boats, can't swim and know you'll get seasick. Think carefully about what you suggest. Would she really want a submarine tour? Will he really enjoy the flower show? If you both have a sincere interest in art, a short walk through the museum is a shared activity that inspires conversation.

Judy agreed to go to a boat show with Joe even though she has no interest in boats and hates large crowds. But he was so enthusiastic it was hard for her to say no. She spent a miserable afternoon, following Joe around as he charged through the milling crowds, pursuing the things that fascinated him. Because she knew nothing about boats, she could only ask questions. Afterwards she realized he would have been better off going alone or with a buddy. Joe didn't need her company. And, in fact, she never heard from him again.

On Patrick's first date with Betty, she asked him to accompany her to a party at a friend's house. The party was almost an hour's drive away and the friends were people Betty had met through her first husband. To make matters worst, most of the guest spoke Spanish and Patrick didn't. He felt awkward and uncomfortable throughout the evening and never contacted Betty again.

Getting ready

What to wear. Maybe it sounds silly to have the same worries as a teen, but you're facing a similar issue — how to make a good first impression. The image you present should be a reflection of you and not someone you'd like to be. Do you have a favorite lucky sweater? Wear whatever puts you at ease. If you're going to meet in an unfamiliar place, visit and check out the dress code in advance.

Remember the basics. Be clean. Shampoo and comb your hair. No spots on your clothes. No shirttails sticking out. No frayed collars and cuffs. No ripped stockings or stained ties. No dark glasses, baseball caps worn backwards, or shorts with white socks and dress shoes. No T-shirts with your grandchildren's picture. No jogging suits. Get the picture?

What message do you want to send? Don't overdress. Leave your gorgeous jewelry at home unless you want to advertise you're wealthy enough to wear your bankbook on your body. Think about your lifestyle and culture. If sporty is your style, let your attire reflect it. If you worry about being too casual, dress up a bit. You'll give the impression you've carefully considered the date and have respect for the process, even if you're only going to spend twenty minutes with someone you'll never see again. Don't wear anything extreme.

When in doubt, choose black. Black is a popular color for clothing because it's background — you get noticed before your clothing. For most people, it's flattering. It makes heavy people look thin and thin folks look elegant. Men: try a black turtleneck sweater with a jacket. This lacks the formality of wearing a tie, yet has a finished look.

Avoid uncomfortable clothing you have to fuss with. You don't want the distraction of wobbling around on stiletto heels or choking on account of a tight collar.

What about glasses? Dark glasses are an absolute no. My friend Marilyn thought of her date as the Lone Ranger because he didn't remove his sunglasses in the restaurant. She couldn't see his eyes. What was he hiding? Wrinkles? Scars? Did he resemble a photo on the Ten-Most-Wanted list?

What about readers? Attractive, inexpensive reading glasses are available. Or you can get glasses with hidden transitions between the reading portion and the rest of the lens. Such glasses mask corrective lenses, a hallmark of aging eyes.

Suppose you don't want to wear reading glasses or bifocals. Visit the restaurant first. Know what you'll order in advance. Calculate the cost and have the money ready, tax included, at the end of the date. Seems like a lot of trouble, but you can do it if you want. Another hint: If you choose not to wear your reading glasses, don't pick up your menu and then adjust the distance so you can read it. Know where you need to hold your menu and place it at that distance. Adjusting calls attention to the need for glasses and your unwillingness to wear them.

Giving and receiving gifts

Should I bring a gift? Most people couldn't imagine asking this question. If you're such a person, feel free to skip this section. But some of us were taught that it is well-bred to bring a token offering. After a phone conversation about books, you might bring the latest novel by your mutually favorite author. Other nice and noncommittal gifts include flowers, candy, or muffins.

In most cases, refrain from giving anything. You don't know this person well enough to predict her reaction. Is she reluctant to take anything from someone she doesn't know? Will she feel bribed to stay at the date longer than the arranged time? Will she feel manipulated into accepting a second date, a bedroom romp, or a marriage proposal? None of the above may be true, but to be on the safe side, hold off on a gift until you can safely assume one is welcome.

Don't accept something you don't want. If it's a pack of chocolates, say thanks. Suppose your date presents you with his complete novel manuscript, all 500 pages of it. If you're interested, you can offer to read the first chapter. Otherwise, simply decline. "I have too many obligations to accept this. I don't have the time and I couldn't do it justice." In particular, don't accept anything you'd feel obliged to return either in person or by mail, if you're not sure you want to meet them again.

We're finally sitting across the table. Now what?

You've managed to arrive at the meeting place looking your best. But now the anxiety sets in. It's easy to lose sight of the reason you're meeting in the first place: it's an opportunity for two people to get to know each other in a friendly way. Remind yourself of your purpose: You're investing a brief time to see if this is a person with whom you can connect. That's all.

Be yourself

Of course you want to present a pleasing presence, but playing a role is detrimental to your goal. For a relationship of any kind to succeed, it must be based on the true personalities of the two participants.

You may find it hard to strike a balance. You want to seem flexible and friendly, but not like a doormat or overly eager to please. You want to appear attractive, but not come across as sexy or brilliant or distant. Such appearances will often achieve the opposite of your desired effect.

You're not applying for a CEO position. Don't oversell. You don't have to prove you're more accomplished and wittier than your date. Some people try to cover up their fear of looking dull by becoming loud and boisterous. If this happens to you, just notice it — you might even want to comment on it. "I realize I'm talking a lot. That's what happens to me when I'm nervous."

I learned this lesson early on. I had a coffee date with a research professor who was not only handsome but distinguished — he had won a number of awards for his scientific accomplishments. This was early in my dating adventures and I thought I needed to impress him at once or I wouldn't get another chance. During our date I practically did a song and dance, recited Shakespeare, sang an aria, and touted all my accomplishments. Know what I mean? We parted and he said he'd be in touch. I must confess I spent the following week anxiously waiting for that call.

He finally phoned on Friday night which I thought was a terrible time since it was much too late to accept a date for the following night. But because I was so interested in him, I decided I'd bend my rules. I was already figuring out what I would wear when he told me "I really enjoyed meeting you and learning so much about your life. But I don't think we're a match. I'm looking for a more, well, *placid* woman. One who has less energy to burn. Maybe we could be friends."

I was so shocked by this rejection that I declined his offer of friendship, another big mistake as I could have met all sorts of interesting people through him. But my feelings were hurt and I wasn't thinking. I had pretended to be someone I wasn't to impress him and it was too late to admit it had been an act. Maybe if I had spent more time with him, as a friend, his false impression might have been corrected.

Trust me: *The only way this will work is to be your everyday self.*

Prepare to listen. Plan to talk only fifty percent about yourself. Above all, keep it light. Here are some suggestions to help ease the tension.

Making conversation

One nice start is to acknowledge your date's willingness to engage in this unsettling endeavor. Thank him for giving it a try. You'll be surprised how conversation flows with minimal effort.

> "Hello. I'm Jeanne. I've been looking forward to our meeting. I'm glad you're willing to give this a try, too! Isn't this a nerve-wracking experience?"

Talk about what you like: books, pets, theater, music, and travel. Follow what you say with a question asking about your date's preferences and experiences. Mention what's good about your life; describing current activities and emphasizing the fullness of your life. Unencumbered? Let your companion know it. Good friends and family? Mention them, but save the details for later. If a topic doesn't catch on, move to something else. You can fall in love with a person even if she doesn't share your fondness for opera but you may never have the chance if you babble on about your favorite arias.

Think of conversation like a tennis game.

You hit the ball, your partner responds and then it's up to the both of you to keep up the volley. Some people are comfortable asking open-ended questions such as what the person is really passionate about or what the happiest day in his life was. Others find these too contrived.

You can ask anything. It hardly matters what you ask as long as you look at the other person and are genuinely curious to hear the answer. Be aware of your date's comfort level with eye contact. A shy person might feel you're staring at him. You'll need to read your companion's body language and be sensitive to his needs.

Try to find connections. The more you can find to agree on, the greater the chance of a second date. It doesn't mean you need to be false or excessively compliant, but the meeting will go smoother if you discover common threads. You may never agree on things more than on your first date, but at least a second date might follow.

The topic of past associations is unavoidable since this is a meeting to explore the possibility of a relationship. If asked, have something nice to say about the last person you were involved with. After all, you did make a commitment to spend a period of your life with her and it says something about your capacity to choose well. Maybe all you can say is that you learned from your mistakes. Then move on to another topic.

Suppose you have a special accomplishment? You've become a skilled painter, or you've been elected leader of an organization, or you are a particularly good seamstress or car mechanic. Mention it so your date can learn about an important part of your character. Since you're only meeting for a short time, your activities shouldn't be the focus of the meeting. Don't bring a copy of your book or a framed painting to demonstrate your competence. If no questions are asked, file that piece of information away. If a question is posed, answer it briefly. Move on to asking some of your own. Show interest. You want to know about the other person. You do not want to play a one-up game. You're offering an appetizer. The main course comes later.

What if your date dominates the conversation? Attentive listening has prime value. He may find it so refreshing to have the opportunity to be heard, he forgets to give you a turn to talk. *No matter,* you say, *my turn will come on the next date.* More times than not, the second date is unlikely to produce a change in focus. A self-absorbed person cannot alter his personality structure sufficiently to be a new person by date two.

Don't let a break in the conversation deter you. Silence can say a lot. It doesn't automatically indicate a lack of interest or a critical attitude. It may represent a pause in which both people reflect about what's going on. Or it may be caused by shyness or lack of recent dating experience. Accept silence as a natural condition.

Give advance thought to what you might do in a quiet period and practice at home. Rehearsals diminish anxiety. Look down at your coffee cup — check out the rim, the bottom, and the sides. It keeps you busy. Don't twist it around or fiddle with things because you're nervous. Look your date in the eyes and smile. After some time has elapsed, break the silence, but don't strain for words. You might ask, "Is this as hard for you as it is for me?"

Asking questions

On a first date, you want to ask questions but you don't want to conduct an interview. Try offering information about a topic you'd like to explore. Tell something about your family and see if the person matches your disclosure. If not, you can say, "And what about your family? Do you have the same issues I do?" Your goal is to establish a dialogue by sharing something about yourself, then asking gentle, non-intrusive questions. Above all, really listen to what the other person says.

I remember my first date with Bruce, a psychologist. I knew from our phone conversations that he was the right age and had been single for a while. Furthermore he liked the same things I did — we were even reading the same book. Because of his qualifications, I skipped the initial coffee date and accepted his invitation to dinner. Usually I'm quite good at asking questions to draw someone out so at first it was a relief that he was the one asking all the questions. But by the end of the meal, I felt a little strange. I knew nothing about him, while he knew quite a lot about me. As we were having dessert he mentioned that he had at least 31 (yes, 31) other women who had answered his ad who he wanted to check out. When he called a few days later to suggest a second date, I turned him down. I didn't enjoy being the object of a psychological evaluation, even though I seemed to have passed the test.

If you ask direct questions, there's always the chance it will feel too intrusive. When were you divorced? How long did your marriage last? Do you see your children often? This is good information to know, just not on a first date. Some people are more private than others. Don't assume your date is secretive or has a lot to hide. She may, but don't come to this conclusion the first time out. You're looking for rapport and not instant intimacy.

There are two vital pieces of information you need to know on or by your first date. Ask, "Is there anyone special in your life *right now?*" If you haven't learned this through e-mail or phone contact, you need to find out soon. It's up to you to pick the moment to pop this question. If your date tells you there is no particular person at the moment, you can follow up by asking how long ago the last relationship ended. If your date just lost a significant person a week ago, she is probably not ready to date. Likewise, you'll need to be cautious if your date says he is in the process of breaking up with his current girlfriend.

The second important question is: How do you spend your day? You want to get some sense of your date's interests and activity level. An unemployed person who lounges the day away in front of the TV is a poor prospect for your future, unless, of course, that's how you like to spend your days.

Answering questions

- How old are you? If you feel uncomfortable answering this question, try answering with your age range. You may get a surprised look, but you've answered the question. Or you can just be honest and say: "I'm sixty-three. If that's a problem for you, I understand." Never lie. You'll have a tough, if not impossible time repairing the damage.
- What do you do for a living? Easy to answer if you're working at something you love, but suppose you've just lost your job and know the chances of finding another one are poor. Talk about your current interests and activities: "I spend my time volunteering, birding, cooking, and bartending." It can be anything as long as you're enthusiastic about it. Find something positive in your life to convey. If you can't, perhaps this isn't a good time to try to find a relationship. You'll be far

more attractive to someone when you're feeling better about yourself. Even if terrible things have happened, you shouldn't offer any details. "Until recently I was working at Company X. I'm not with them now. It was time for a change." Then talk about the things you're actually doing.

- Why have you never married? Here are some possible answers: "It was by choice. My work life was fulfilling for a long time. But now I've decided I'd like to share my life with someone else." "I've never found the right person." "The great love of my life died in Vietnam."

- Have you had cosmetic surgery? "We don't know each other well enough to share private information yet!" (Chances are if someone has the gall to ask you this on the first date, you'll never share anything else, except maybe the bill for your coffee.) You might try a simple, "No." That one word response is a real showstopper.

- What do you think about sex? Worse than the question about plastic surgery. What you think about sex is private. "We don't know each other well enough to share private information yet!" Don't even start to share your opinions —

you'll be opening a Pandora's box of troubles.

- What do you think of me? You're asked what you think of the other person before you've had a chance to catch your breath and add sugar to your coffee. Don't say anything negative for safety reasons.
- What do you weigh? Gross. But be honest if this person is someone you want to see again. This question may ward off possible problems in the future.
- What did your ex-husband do for a living? "It's not an issue." Or "I don't talk about that."
- Why did your marriage break up? "I ended it and didn't look back." This or some variation of the response shows you're not about to elaborate; yet it doesn't make you look evasive. "It just didn't work out." "You know, that was a long time ago. It's water under the bridge now."
- Do you have any STD's? What a turnoff. The message is "Hey, cookie. Forget that relationship stuff. How about sex?" Again use some variation on "I think it's too soon to talk about something that personal."
- Are you in good health? Also a little forward for a first date. "I'll answer, but I wonder why you're asking me now?"

- How much money do you earn? "Why do you ask?" Don't answer if you don't want to.
- Where do you live? "We'll talk about that when we get to know each other better."

Topics to avoid

Keep the conversation light. You cannot predict where the dialogue will go, but you can keep it from going in an uncomfortable direction. It's equally important to emphasize what shouldn't be discussed in a first meeting.

Certain information is better left unshared. There is a fine line between being evasive and being firm about what you're uncomfortable about revealing for the moment.

Here are some guidelines:

- Avoid detailing your romantic and marital history. No matter how angry you are at your last love, this isn't the time to describe her shortcomings and how you've been wronged. Nor is this the time to describe how glorious things were with your deceased partner. Your date wants to be the focus of your interest.

- Don't imply a relationship already exists by asking, "How was your day?" You don't know this person and requesting such details is prematurely intimate.
- Steer clear of sweeping generalizations about the opposite gender. Remember, the person in front of you is included in the put down.
- No verbal sparring matches. Don't get into a heated debate about globalization or why tear gas isn't an effective means to deal with protesters. Avoid discussing politics.
- No mention of health issues. Your body and its functioning are personal. Don't say a word about your troublesome prostate, the miseries of menopause, or the workings of your bowels.
- A health question may arise if you have a newly diagnosed condition or a serious chronic one. Is it important to reveal this on a first date? Opinions vary. You want to avoid anything that smacks of deception and you believe a potential companion has every right to know. But it doesn't have to be in the first half hour. After a person gets to know you and likes you, she is more likely to be tolerant of what seems an insurmountable problem.
- Pass up talking about a recent disaster in

your personal life. This person you're sitting with may be a future ally, but it's too much to expect on the first date. Reschedule if you cannot give your companion full attention for the half hour.

- Don't be rude. Don't criticize the waiter. Don't criticize your date.
- Don't offer compliments no matter how justified. "How do you manage to stay so slim?" isn't a question to ask at this time. Nor should you mention your companion's adorable goatee.
- Don't belittle yourself or your accomplishments. "All I do is work so I haven't had time to meet someone." You don't need to tell someone you don't date very much or you haven't had a date in three years.
- Gossip is out. Don't talk about other people's problems no matter how important or interesting. Your date needs to know about you and not your grandchildren's accomplishments, your daughter's messy divorce or your best friend's allergies.
- No confessions. Intimacy can't be forced by revealing how you tolerated your ex-husband's abusiveness or your son's recent arrest.
- Don't discuss your therapy, religious ex-

periences, or recovery program. This information is too intimate for a first date and you don't want to come away feeling judged or criticized.

- Sex is unmentionable.
- No touching. Don't assume you can hug, hold hands, or put your arm around your companion's shoulder. You don't want to get rejected or decked. Wait until there is an unambiguous invitation for physical contact. You can't possibly know the nuances of your date's signals, since you don't know your date. Be patient. You'll have another chance on your second date.

Signs of danger

There is a difference between clues and danger signals. It's easy to ignore clues. It's not as easy to ignore danger signs. One clue isn't enough to negate seeing this person again. They have to add up. Make a list to get a clearer picture. Here are some clues that should get your attention:

- You can't seem to get a word in. Everything is about the other person. He tells you about his past and his hopes for the future. You hear funny stories, descriptions of work, and family. Yet somehow, as charmed as you may be, you realize you might as well not be there. Is this a warning of what your future relationship might be like? Or is this someone who is nervous and anxious to make a good impression? How does this person react when you interrupt and tell something about yourself?

- Your date drinks two beers and four scotches during dinner and then has an after-dinner cognac, then suggests adjourning to the cocktail lounge for a drink.
- The person bad-mouths all her past boyfriends.
- The person complains about being bored. He or she is looking for someone to fill gaps in his life.
- Your date looks bored right now.
- You're hearing more than you want about a subject such as finances or the lack of them, previous bad luck in dating, family troubles, and health issues.
- You're hearing more than you want about a subject of no interest to you, such as stamp collecting and you can't get the topic to shift.
- You feel criticized.

- You feel bored.
- You feel uneasy, but can't identify why.
- You find the person so unattractive you know you won't want to get closer even if you get to know her and find out she is a wonderful person.
- All you can think about is getting back to the book you were reading before you left home.
- The person is distracted by other people or pictures on the wall.
- The person discloses too much too soon and sets up an instant romantic connection, creating a false sense of intimacy.

Despite these clues, you may want to see this person again. It's your choice, but be alert to the fact that trouble may be on the way.

Safety first

Don't give out your address or phone number unless you're absolutely sure of your date's impeccable credentials. In the case of a fix-up, this means you've verified the connection through mutual and trusted acquaintances.

I made this mistake twice. The first time

I gave my phone number to a man I met on an Internet dating site. He was divorced, lived in a good part of town and had similar interests to mine so I wasn't concerned. But as soon as I gave him my number he started calling me every few minutes. We hadn't even met in person yet he was acting like we had a relationship. He might have been a great guy but his lack of boundaries and neediness were not attractive.

It was annoying and took some effort to get him to stop calling but it wasn't scary, unlike the second guy. He seemed fine too — he was a lawyer and had been introduced to me by a medical colleague. However, he called and demanded to see me sooner than I was ready. When I turned him down he got angry. The next time he called he sounded paranoid. He asked, "What do you have against me?" and seemed threatening. I was so uncomfortable, I changed my phone number and learned my lesson. Keep your phone number private until you've met at least more than once and feel safe in giving out this personal information.

If you feel uneasy during a date, you can leave at any time. You need no excuse. You can end with a simple, "We need to stop here. I think we've both given this a try, but I feel we're not a match. I wish you the best, but I'm going to leave now." You don't even need to say that much if you feel frightened: just get up and go. Since you met in a public setting, you can alert a waitperson or manager of your distress and request to be seen safely to your car.

If your coffee date turns into a dinner date, it should never, never become a sleepover or wind up with sex on the menu.

Who pays?

If your first date is a brief meeting where the expected activity is to drink a beverage and talk, get the relationship off on the right foot by sharing the whole activity. If you arrive first, wait until your date appears to purchase your drink.

Society's attitude towards who pays the check is fluid. If a man pays, does this make the woman feel cherished and nurtured? Does it imply a caretaking role? Or could it be simply a polite gesture from a time when this was the norm? If a man doesn't pay, does that mean he's selfish? Is he a good provider? Is he stingy? If a woman doesn't volunteer to pay her share, is it a signal she will be high maintenance? Thirty years ago it was obligatory for men to pick up the bill for everything from coffee to the rent. In the past there was an implied meaning in men paying for joint activities. Today it's hard to say what it means.

Decide what makes you feel comfortable, but be flexible. Don't draw too many conclusions on the first date. Some men and women over fifty have updated their perspectives. You won't know how your companion feels about money until you get to know him.

It's safe to assume each of you will purchase your own coffee. Men are definitely not obligated to pay for women. If you've been at a restaurant with table service, it's polite for the woman to ask, "What's my share?" when the bill arrives or to reach for her purse to indicate she's ready to pay. If the woman reaches for her wallet when the check appears and the man says, "Allow me," then the appropriate response is "Thank you." You're accepting a latte not a Lexus. If the woman likes the man and want to see him again, she can add, "The next coffee is on me." She sends two messages: she's generous and wants to get together again.

Ending the date

A date can end in several outcomes. You both like each other and you're enthusiastic about the future; one person thinks it's a go while the other wants to move on; both of you know you'll pass; or someone is unsure and wants to think things over. Each option takes some skill to enact smoothly. Be prepared.

Mutual Interest: If you want to see the other person again, it's important to give that message. Second dates often don't happen because there isn't a loud and clear signal that another meeting is desired. This happens especially with older people who haven't been dating for a while. You don't have to be forward and thrust your business card at the person. You can say, "I had a really nice time. I'm glad we met. Thanks for the coffee and the company. I look forward to the next time we get together." Look pleasant and enthusiastic, but don't ask when this is going to happen. It might or it might not. You just want to indicate your interest.

If you're a woman and don't want to wait for the man to initiate contact, you can add, "Let's keep in touch. Why don't you give me a call?" Or "I'll get in touch with you." A man might say, "I'll be glad to give you my number and you can give me a call if you want to get together again or, if you'd like, I'll be glad to call you. Whichever feels most comfortable for you."

Should women call men after the first date? In an article on dating in *Cosmopolitan*, a magazine for women in their twenties, the writer advises the woman to show

> *"If you feel uneasy during a date, you can leave at any time. You need no excuse."*

her interest by calling to set a second date. But I think women of our generation should wait and see what happens. As a rule, men don't expect to be called. It's safer in the beginning to follow the old-fashioned guidelines until you know the other person's expectations.

Should a woman call or e-mail the next day just to say she's had a good time and enjoyed the meeting? I still believe we should stick with the norms for our generation for now, but if you have a powerful inclination to initiate contact, go ahead. The earth will not open up and swallow you if this turns out to be a mistake.

Men, if you're so inclined, call or e-mail

the next day to say you had a nice time and you'll be in touch to set up another meeting. If you'd like a second date, don't allow too much time to elapse before your next contact or the process will lose momentum. Call or e-mail within the week, even if your schedule doesn't permit another get-together in the very near future.

Suppose at first you weren't interested, but later, after some consideration, you change your mind. Or maybe you put off making the call because you wondered what reception you would get. Go ahead and call, even if a few weeks have elapsed. Honesty is endearing when you explain, "I wanted to call you, but I was too nervous to do it."

One-sided Interest: You didn't have a good time and don't want a second date. But your companion thinks you're great. "Would you like to do this again sometime?" he says with great enthusiasm. "How about getting together next Friday or Saturday or, if you can't make it then, maybe Tuesday?" Remember, this half hour is exploratory and you aren't keen on what you found. Don't lie.

You want to respectfully convey you don't consider this a match. Don't preface your remarks with a comment about what a nice time you had or how wonderful it was to meet him. Say something like, "I'm glad we had the opportunity to meet." (You are telling the truth. You are pleased that the opportunity occurred, even if you're not enthused by this person.) "I'm afraid this just isn't a match. We both tried. You know there are no guarantees. I wish you the best in your search." This has a ring of finality to it. You want to close the door. Your date might protest: "But I had such a great time. Couldn't we give it another try?" Simply say: "No. This doesn't feel like a match to me. I wish you the best in your search." Do not be coerced into another meeting. Don't offer even a whiff of encouragement when you're sure it's hopeless.

Be open-minded, but don't feel obligated to force yourself to like someone. One of my teachers used to say, "You can get a horse to drink whiskey, but you can't make him like it."

Mutual disinterest: You feel like leaving five minutes into the experience. Maybe you've been misled. The person looks like they need a bath more than a date. Or her comments are offensive. Maybe you don't like the look in his eyes. Or she seems more interested in watching the barista than in talking to you.

A half hour can seem an eternity with the wrong person sitting across the table. Yes, you have permission to get up and go. You both had the best intentions, even if it doesn't seem that way. Maybe the other person knew it was a long shot but gave it his best. Don't be rude, even if you feel totally shortchanged. "I wish you the best, but this doesn't feel right so I'm leaving." Go immediately.

Uncertainty: You're asked if you want to get together again and you're not sure. You'd like to consider it. It's fine to say, "It sounds like a good idea but I want to think it over. I'll give you a call (or e-mail)." Do follow through. If you opt against another date, write or call to say you've thought things over, but you've decided you're not a match. There is no need to give any reasons. You never need to justify your feelings. If there are definite reasons, will it really help the person to know she's too short or not in your economic bracket?

Don't say, "I'll call," as a polite way to end a date if you don't intend to call. This isn't fair. Be ready with several alternative phrases to make a smooth transition.

And just because you've heard the parting phrase, "I'll call," don't take this as gospel. It is often used as filler to ease the discomfort of ending a date. Maybe you would never dream of making such a promise without keeping it. But you have no way of knowing your date's ethics.

Do you shake hands? My inclination is not to do so. Hand shaking is a symbol of formality used in a business endeavor. Also, you don't have any indication of how your companion feels about physical contact. It's safer to refrain from physical contact during your first meeting. If your date reaches out and touches your arm or shoulder, I would, if interested, respond with a smile and the statement, "I had a nice time. I'm looking forward to getting together again."

Thinking It Over

Although this is a half hour coffee date, you need to remember your criteria. When you get home, examine the list you made about what you cannot tolerate.

Sabrina met Woodrow at the restaurant near her house for coffee and dessert on a weekday afternoon. They were only one year apart in age, and she liked the fact that he was short — she wouldn't have to stand on a chair to look him in the eyes.

He told fascinating anecdotes about his travels and apparently had a thriving investment business. But during their conversation he kept asking about her sexual preferences, even though she declined to discuss this subject. When she got home, she realized the vague feeling of creepiness she felt outweighed his seeming assets.

Keep in mind that you want to determine if you like your date as much, if not more, than she likes you. You don't need to sell yourself. Think of your effort in terms of evaluating the other person for seventy-five percent of the time and being evaluated for twenty-five percent of the time. Remember, you do have control.

Did your date present well? If you walk to his car and have the opportunity to look inside, is it clean on first glance or do you see fast food wrappers strewn on the floor? Was she sufficiently respectful to appear tidy and well groomed? Is he appropriately unwilling to reveal personal information to a stranger by saying "I'd rather not say," or "I'll tell you that when we know each other better." Or is he evasive and indirect?

I had a first date with a man named Bernard who sounded good on the phone. He said he was a teacher although he was vague about what he taught. We met for

coffee and he seemed presentable, although he hadn't been divorced very long.
I was still mulling over whether or not I
wanted to meet him again as we walked
out into the parking lot where he proudly
pointed out his battered blue VW van with
a yellow hound dog rattling the window
and barking. He said that he and his dog
were living in it "until they could get an
apartment." No second date for Bernard.

Your goal on the first date is to learn
enough to decide if you want a second date
with this person. The information you
gather over the next few dates will tell you
if this person has the character traits you
want in a potential mate. Don't try to cram
a lifetime of information into half an hour!

7

Great Expectations

You've jumped the biggest hurdle: you've survived the first date. Now the hard work begins. A wise friend told me her rule: she doesn't start talking about her new prospect until after the third date. But this is difficult. When you meet someone you want to see again, it's easy to start dreaming about the future.

Ups and downs go with the territory. Will he call again? Will she want to go out with me once she learns my history and faults? Each phase of the dating process has its own perils and rewards.

Once past the first date, dating is an exploratory process, during which you get to know each other. You're not yet in the courtship phase where there's a spoken or implied sense that at least one of the partners would like to make the relationship permanent. As time goes on, you'll decide if you've developed sufficient trust to want to proceed further.

Dating is more than a cup of coffee and less than signing a lease. To experience this stage to the fullest, you need time. This is a process that can't be rushed no matter how pressed you feel at this point in your life.

I've noticed that getting to know someone seems to have four distinct phases:

- The first three dates. If you get past that, and you're still interested, it's safe to rave to friends about the color of his eyes or her sense of humor. At that point, you can officially think of yourself as "going out" with someone.
- After three months, you've probably shared a lot of information and many activities. The romantic side of your relationship is still fresh and new and you've had the opportunity to spend time alone and with family and friends. This is another point at which to evaluate whether or not to continue.
- Six and nine months are good milestones at which to take stock. You have shared holidays and special events.
- The final dating milestone often comes at the one-year mark. You've had the chance to experience life together

through four seasons. The glow of the new has worn off and reality sets in. You've gone through a round of celebrations and vacations. You have probably had some tough times and maybe an experience with ill health. This is a particularly good juncture to decide whether or not you want to continue.

Emotional baggage

Expect the dating process to go slowly. As an older person, you may be more sensitive or more vulnerable than when you were younger. Be kind to yourself and honest with your partner.

You have the experience of a lifetime behind you so you may find it easier to identify emotional issues from the past. That doesn't mean, however, that you won't repeat destructive patterns.

One of my clients, Mario, a 63 year old lawyer, knew he had a problem with demanding women. His first two wives took advantage of his ample income and generous nature to accumulate glamorous wardrobes, expensive possessions, and luxurious homes. Even his two college-age daughters knew how to manipulate their dad. All they had to do was smile at him and he'd give them whatever they asked for.

When Mario first met Alice, he was sure he had finally found a different sort of woman. Alice wore baggy jeans, lived comfortably on her pension, and showed no interest in draining his resources. Yet after a month of dating, Mario noticed she was always criticizing him. She didn't like the way he dressed. She complained he wasn't attentive enough. She insisted they go to the San Juan Islands for their first vacation together when he was looking forward to Cancun. She was even bossy in bed. Mario's wallet was safe, but not his psyche.

Mario was dismayed that despite his careful planning, he had picked yet another woman who bossed him around. He told me: "My mother always dressed to kill and was always after my dad for more money, more time, and even more kids. My wives were carbon copies of my mother. But I thought I was safe with Alice." But Mario had been relying too much on external cues and not enough on the psychological dynamics between the two of them. And so he ended up with yet another forceful, demanding woman, albeit one who wore athletic shoes instead of stiletto heels.

Years of experience can't erase the un-conscious desire to play out parts of our childhood emotional drama. We don't do this to torture ourselves. It's a natural at-tempt to find a more satisfying conclusion to an old story. Understanding the subtle and elusive dynamics of our patterns is a complex task. It's even harder to figure them out when you're in the middle of a new romance.

How do we change? Making different choices is one way. If you've always gone out with charming but angry men, you might want to date that mild mannered ac-countant. But sometimes, this sort of change is superficial. Take time to reflect. If you see yourself hurtling down an all-too-familiar road, get off before you've in-vested too much time and energy.

Dating is a chance to get to know your partner. Embrace the difficulties as well as the pleasures. Can you solve problems to-gether? Will you support each other through tough times? Can you be intimate and still maintain a comfortable emotional distance? You won't learn this in a few eve-nings or after spending the night together but you'll gradually accumulate this infor-mation after months of sharing experiences and conversations.

Even if you think you've finally found your soulmate, go slowly. In fact, the more head over heels you are, the more slowly you should proceed. During the first flush of romance, you sometimes overlook the clues of trouble. As you go along, pursue any issues that bother you. For instance, if you find out he has children, but doesn't see them, ask questions. Don't ignore anything. You want to gather as much information as possible before you get too deeply involved.

After the first date

As discussed in the previous chapter, it's important to be clear at the end of the first date about whether or not you'd like to meet again. But suppose you're interested and you thought your date knew that, but you haven't heard from him.

Perhaps he already gave you the message nonverbally. Did he avoid eye contact at the end of the date? Did he say he enjoyed meeting you but nothing else? Perhaps you failed to make your interest clear. Did you say you'd like to get together again? Did you trade phone numbers or e-mail addresses?

Whatever you do, don't sit by the phone

waiting for it to ring. You probably remember the agony of that experience from your younger years. How you jumped every time the phone rang, then rushed through the call if it wasn't from the person you expected. How you made excuses: maybe she lost the phone number, maybe he was in a terrible automobile accident, hooked to a breathing machine in the ICU. You may think you're too old to go through this again, but desire and disappointment don't disappear with age.

Should you call? If you're a man, yes. If you're a woman, I suggest, on the basis of my experience and those of friends, you rein in your impatience and keep your hands off that phone. In our generation, the man is expected to take the initiative. Although you have a perfect right to call, you may not like the results. A shy man might be scared by your eagerness, an old-fashioned man might be offended by your impertinence and a more direct man might simply tell you he hasn't called because he's not interested.

It's hard, but keep this important fact in mind: if you don't get a call, it's not you! Maybe you look like someone from his past who treated him badly. Perhaps she prefers men she can dominate intellectually. If it's not a match, it's not a match. Think of dating as a process rather than focusing on each individual experience.

What sort of relationship do you want?

After 50 your needs and wishes may be different than they were when you were younger. Having experienced various types of relationships over the past years, you know your limitations and your preferences. Don't assume that dating has to lead to marriage, monogamy or living together.

At age 64, Lorna was just beginning to enjoy her independence. She loved her condo, her cat, and occasional visits with her grandchildren. When her husband divorced her, after 42 years of marriage, she felt mostly relief. She was tired of being ignored, tired of sitting across the breakfast table from a man who thought the *New York Times* was more interesting than talking to her. She enjoyed the peace of her solitary life, with no one around to please or impress.

When she met Ed, she relished every minute she spent with him — he loved to talk and he was interested in her opinions and ideas. Yet she didn't want to see him at the breakfast table every morning. Weekends together were wonderful but they were enough. Although she couldn't imagine life without Ed, she also couldn't imagine giving up her condo, her cat, and most important, her independence.

Nora in Milwaukee and Carlos in Madrid find satisfaction in a relationship that exists only in cyberspace. Both in their fifties, they met on the Internet. They flirted via e-mail and traded pictures and life stories. New Year's was wonderful. They chatted on the Internet and toasted each other with glasses of champagne. At first they planned to meet but over time, their enthusiasm waned. Nora had little interest in having another lover and Carlos had been burned too many times in the past. Nora couldn't imagine ever living in Spain and Carlos, who specialized in Spanish commercial law, knew he couldn't use his skills outside his own country. Both felt guilty about enjoying the limitations imposed by a four-thousand mile gap but it was easy to forget

> *"Dating is a chance to get to know your partner. Embrace the difficulties as well as the pleasures."*

they were so far apart when the next e-mail arrived.

Perhaps you want a relationship without physical intimacy. That's fine too. For many older people, companionship is more important than sex.

Relationships, like friendships, can be custom crafted to meet your needs. If you know what you want, be honest about it as soon as it's comfortable to do so. This saves disappointment later. If your prospective partner tells you she will never give up her tiny studio, pay attention. If your date talks about his dreams of marriage while you feel allergic at the thought, say so early. It's safe to assume your partner is telling the truth. Think about whether or not you can accept his/her goal and modify your own. Don't assume your companion will magically change once you're a couple.

When do you tell someone your dreams? This is a delicate question. Every case is unique, but I can say with certainty: not on the first date. As time goes on, if these topics don't come up naturally, you might want to raise them. Don't put off discussing them for fear you won't like the answers. Carrying the weight of an unasked question can be a burden too heavy for any relationship to withstand.

What to talk about

Whatever you say, let it be the truth. Lying ultimately makes a mess. Besides, it's hard to keep track of lies. It's easier to remember what you said if you tell the truth. If, after the fifth or fifteenth date, you don't want to discuss certain aspects of your life, simply say: "I'd rather not talk about that." Omissions are fine, but embellishing or altering details is risky.

Address issues that irritate you. Don't ignore your concerns. This may be difficult if you've spent your life holding back your feelings for fear of being seen as demanding or critical. Now is the time to try new behavior. Practice. Tell yourself that the next time a distressing situation arises, you're going to say something.

When you hold back your feelings, you run the risk that your resentments will accumulate, perhaps triggering an emotional explosion. Yet, in the heat of the moment you may say things you later regret. I use a twenty-four hour rule. If something bothers me, I wait until the next day before I say something. If I still feel strongly then I express my concerns. Issues get stale and less immediate after a day has gone by. If you postpone your grievances much longer that twenty-four hours, you give the impression that you secretly harbor anger. Speak within the day or let it go. Most likely a similar situation will arise in the future and you'll have another chance.

Exception: If someone is rude to you then it's best to say something on the spot. The most appropriate response is some version of "Get lost."

Consider your "relationship parameters," a more tasteful notion than "rules." Let's look at the issue of who calls whom and how often. Be clear about your preferences and ask directly for what you want. For instance, "I really like it when you call me. Would it be okay for me to call you?" If you're getting too many calls, you might say: "I need some private time. It feels too early in our relationship to speak every day." Discuss and establish parameters that work for both of you. If your date won't accept these guidelines, you might want to reconsider this relationship.

Shelley was charmed by Arnold's good looks, generous spirit, and impeccable manners. But only six weeks into dating, she began to worry about his desire to spend every minute of every day with her. She wanted to see him only on weekends but Arnold wanted to see her every night of the week. At the end of an evening, she had a hard time getting him out the door. Even when they agreed he would leave at 11, since she had to get up early the next day, he would linger, charming her with anecdotes and jokes. He even tried to talk to her while she was taking a shower. Shelley finally broke up with him because he didn't respect her needs.

Talk about what words and actions mean to you. What does "I love you" imply? What does it mean to go out with the same person every Saturday night? What does it mean to introduce your date to your grandchildren? What does having sex mean to you? Avoid ambivalence. Don't make assumptions. Subjects are for discussion and not argument. You're sharing information. If you don't like the answer you get, file it away for later consideration. Don't draw your conclusions too soon.

> *"If, after the fifth or fifteenth date, you don't want to discuss certain aspects of your life, simply say: 'I'd rather not talk about that.'"*

Speak about your fears and ask your companion about his or hers. Just listen. Don't try to soothe another's doubts by offering immediate reassurance. This can only happen after you establish trust. If you have something painful to share, be clear that you're not asking for help. Say, "I have some things to tell you, but I don't want to discuss them. I'd just like you to listen." Watch your date's response. Does he look directly at you while listening? Does he look bored or irritated? The response to a sensitive subject gives a world of information about a person.

Talk about how you envision your future. I used to think that raising this subject was too pushy until I noted that my younger patients and the medical students with whom I work are comfortable talking about relationship goals. They are open and direct about their plans for marriage and children. So it's certainly reasonable for you to ask similar questions. Do you foresee living with someone again? Are you interested in marriage? Or do you see yourself dating, but maintaining a separate life? Again at this stage, you're just gathering information, but obviously your goals should be similar if you're going to make a relationship work in the long run.

When you have an issue to address, keep it simple. Don't deluge your companion with complaints. "There's something I'd like to talk about. It makes me feel uncomfortable when you answer your cell phone and have long conversations while we're out to dinner." Be ready with how you would like to see the problem solved and be sure it is realistic. Don't ask for a change in personality. You won't get it.

What not to talk about

The less said about the past, the better for both partners. No one forgets his or her past, but it does no good to rehash old hurts. Don't ask for details of previous romantic relationships. If you do ask a question, keep it open-ended. "How did things go between you?" Listen to the story, but don't pry.

It is important for your partner to know what works and doesn't work for you. Rather than telling him how often Charlie kept you waiting, raise the topic of being on time. "It really upsets me when you're late. Please call me if you can't be at my house at the time we've set." This is a much better strategy. Your new romantic interest will not be tempted to take Charlie's part against you. Convey your feelings and spell out what you need to feel comfortable.

Never describe past sexual experiences, especially better performances or firmer bodies. It will only make your partner anxious, an emotion guaranteed to inhibit good sex.

Talking about "Our Relationship" can be a bore. By the time we're past 50, most of us have had enough. Some discussion is necessary and too much is dreary. After the first few months, limit yourself to occasional "check-ins" to ask, "How do you think things are going?"

Don't criticize. Don't analyze. Maybe you believe you know why your partner behaves a certain way. Maybe you're certain a particular childhood experience or early trauma was to blame. Suppose your partner wants you to call every night, and you're certain it's because her father left when she was three. Don't point this out. If you really believe your girlfriend suffers from insecurity, do what you can to help her feel more secure. But remember, you're not her therapist.

Suppose your date asks for too much too soon? Follow your instincts. As soon as you feel a boundary is crossed, put on the brakes. "I'm not ready to talk about this yet. I'd rather wait until we get to know each other better." This is respectful and honest. You're not criticizing your companion for being too intrusive, but you're letting your feelings be known. Watch and listen for the response. Perhaps your date was anxious to connect. If he takes your gentle reminder gracefully, perhaps with a bit of embarrassment, that's fine. If he persists with the line of questioning that made you nervous, it's better to know this early.

The grey zone

You're now spending time together. You want to know more about the person you're with. Contrary to advice you may get elsewhere, I feel you can ask any question you want, except about sex.

Go ahead and ask if he has ever spent any time in jail. Perhaps you'll get into an interesting discussion about Vietnam war protests; perhaps you'll learn you're dating someone with a history of assault. You also will want to know about your prospective partner's health, any financial and emotional responsibilities assumed before you met, and what your date does in terms of work and social life.

However, don't ask questions like a census collector checking off the boxes on a tally sheet. Use good sense and ask when the moment seems right. If someone doesn't want to answer a question, let it go. You don't do any harm by asking in a thoughtful, respectful way.

Do I want this to continue?

Once the dating process begins, it can assume a life of its own. Remember, you can control how things go. Whether you've pledged undying love or just arranged to go out next Saturday night, you have the prerogative to change your mind. You don't even need a good reason. At any point along the road you can decide to stop.

Don't be forced or bullied. Don't keep a date under threat. And don't feel guilty if you change your mind.

Signs of trouble

- Your date is a loner. At first she made an effort to appear social. She speaks about friends, but she never goes out with any and no one ever calls her. She says very little about past relationships. If you're looking for someone with a capacity to connect and contribute to a social life, this is not the person for you. Unless, of course, you are also an introvert and crave someone similar.

- Your date meticulously avoids talking about the future, or worse, tantalizes you with conversations about the trips you'll take together and social events you'll attend. After a while you realize nothing ever happens. Fantasy talk is intoxicating, but leaves you feeling empty and misled.
- The relationship is all about the other person. Conversation never includes what you've done today. She decides what you do whenever you get together. You can't redirect the topic. With a narcissist across the table, you might get a few minutes to talk about your interests, but don't expect your companion to listen. This relationship will only work if you like being the admiring support person for someone who has to be the center of attention.

Signs of disrespect

If you're not treated with respect early on, chances are you'll never get better treatment. Your date is likely to be on good behavior at the start, but over time the façade will slip. What are signs of lack of respect?

- Your concerns aren't taken seriously.
- You're stood up for a date with no call or no explanation.
- You plan to go to a formal event and your date shows up in jeans.
- When you say you want to discuss something important, your date says "later" and never brings up the topic again.
- When you talk about something important that happened to you, your date either belittles or ignores you.
- Your date is rude to the waiter.
- Your date belittles your family or friends.

Taking time off

It just doesn't feel right. Maybe it feels too good to be true. Those bouquets of flowers, cute messages, and gourmet dinners seem too perfect. Believe me: if it feels too good to be true, it probably is. Follow your instincts, even if all of your friends think you've found a winner. Ask for a time-out. "It's been good spending time with you, but this is going a little too fast for me. I need a break. I'll get in touch after a while. If you meet someone else in the meantime, I'll understand. It's the chance I'll take." This is hard to do, but after some time away from the person you might identify what made you uneasy. If it's just the jitters, call again. Perhaps you'll be able to resume where you left off. You take a chance with this strategy but it's worth taking if your future happiness is at stake.

Corliss was Marilyn's dream man. They met on an Internet dating site and had their first in person date within two weeks. Soft-spoken and secure, he was a retired professor of sociology who still maintained an office on campus, thanks to his emeritus status. He cultivated bonsai trees as a hobby and gave Marilyn an expensive book on the topic to introduce her to his interest. But he didn't neglect her interests — he gave her a recording of her favorite symphony. She enjoyed their quiet dinners and time spent cuddling on the couch.

So she couldn't quite figure out why she felt uneasy about their relationship. She decided to take a break and think things over. She had been swept off her feet and needed a breather. Meanwhile, she decided to learn more about Corliss. She called a friend who knew someone who had taught in the same department as Corliss. "Nasty old curmudgeon," was the friend's comment. "Everyone was glad when he retired, but especially the female grad students. He was always pinching their bottoms."

Perhaps there's nothing wrong with your date. Perhaps you're the one feeling out of sorts. Maybe the prospect of dating and falling in love again was exciting. But now you're not so sure you're ready. Even if your last breakup was five years ago, there's no timetable for grieving. Perhaps the new person can't match your memories of your past partner. Maybe you feel like you're betraying the person you lost. Or you compiled a list of unreasonable requirements that can never be met. For whatever reason, you thought you were ready but you're not.

If you're feeling unsure, remember you can end the relationship at any time. It's best to do so with clarity and respect. "I'm not feeling ready to pursue this relationship seriously at this time. I'm sorry. I thought I was ready and I've enjoyed spending time with you but I'm going to end this now."

Some of these issues can be addressed.

But with such a serious subject you can't expect to find an easy ten-step solution in a self-help book. This is the time to consider: would it be better to wait until you resolve some issues rather than forge ahead?

Your partner wants a time out

What should you do if you've been dating for several months and your partner asks for space? For one thing, don't argue about it. You might be disappointed but you can appreciate the rationale. Theoretically, during a trial separation, your prospective partner recognizes your value, thus inspiring a new round of enthusiasm for dating. But this is not the only possibility. Often such a request is an attempt to end the relationship gently.

If you do resume the relationship, you may learn the person was seeing someone else and you'll have to deal with that. My advice? Don't let yourself "dangle." Move on. Put your energy into meeting someone new.

Suppose your partner suggests dating other people, perhaps with a line like this: "It'll help us know if we really want to be together." This is either a sign of uncertainty about you or interest in another. If this sounds fine to you, go ahead — just don't take the relationship too seriously. But if you prefer dating one person at a time, don't go along with this scheme. Simply move on and fine someone whose goal is the same as yours.

Sometimes contact abruptly ends. After several happy months, your date suddenly drops off the face of the earth. Your e-mails and phone calls go unanswered. You start to worry. Was he in a car wreck? Did she have a heart attack? Or maybe you had one disagreement and then he disappeared. You wonder if you said the wrong thing. You review that last phone call trying to determine what offended her.

Sometimes your date will reappear and want to pick up where you left off. You may be overjoyed at the second chance, but such behavior should be a red flag.

Maybe you will eventually learn the reason your date disappeared. Maybe you will get her on the phone and she'll say she needed some space. Maybe it's better that you don't know.

Even though Marilyn had heard some negative things about Corliss, she decided to give him another chance. After all, she had only heard one person's opinion and she could blame the colleague's nastiness on the sort of backbiting common in a university department.

But although Corliss seemed happy to resume their relationship, they went out less frequently. He also called less often and finally stopped calling altogether. Marilyn left several messages which he didn't return. Finally she got him in person.

"What's wrong?" she asked. "Why are you avoiding me?"

"Stop hassling me," he said. "I'm not interested in you. You're too old for me." Perhaps it would have been better for Marilyn if she didn't know why he stopped calling.

Finances

You've spent the greater part of your life managing your money, either well or poorly. Whatever you're done, you've done it on your own, or with previous partners. When you begin dating, you must also deal with your date's beliefs and attitudes towards money.

Address financial values and differences

early on. Take a look at how things are going. Do you have an easy time deciding who pays for dates? Can you discuss this topic? If you haven't spoken about this, is it because your date is uncomfortable talking about money?

Who pays can be a persistent source of discomfort. Like people in any age category, people over 50 have various financial situations. Some men and women have substantial means; others are living on fixed incomes. Sometimes one person offers to pay on the first date to make a good impression, but hopes the other person will reciprocate by covering the next one. A second date is a good time for a short discussion about money. You don't have to bring along your financial records. Just say something like, "You paid last time; my treat this time." If the person declines and grabs the check, let it be.

If your date is adamant about always paying, there's probably a reason. As long as it doesn't violate your ethics or principles, go along with it. But you need to make an offer, even if it's always refused. This shows the subject of money isn't taboo and the other person can introduce it at any time.

Perhaps there's an inequality of finances. A man who looks comfortable may actually be hurting. Perhaps he is making one or more alimony payments, paying tuition for college or supporting a grandchild. A woman who dresses nicely and lives in an elegant home, may be on food stamps.

Have a chat as early as possible. Say something simple and succinct, for instance, "I've really been enjoying the things we do together. How would you like to share the expenses?" It will make you feel more like a potential couple if you can talk about such an everyday yet significant issue. Opening up the discussion will let you know where you and your companion stand on the subject.

Whatever works for both of you is fine. A woman may prefer to be treated financially; it may represent caring in both a symbolic and actual manner. And some men prefer women who enjoy this role. If it's a match, then great. But you do need to find out where you are in the financial preference spectrum.

Gifts

Issues of money easily lead to a discussion of gifts. The longer you date, the more likely it is that you'll exchange gifts.

You have a lifetime of traditions and so does the person you're getting to know. Find out in advance of a holiday what your date likes. Perhaps she hates shopping for gifts, especially during the Christmas rush, and will be relieved to know that you prefer an evening out instead of a purchased gift. Perhaps he will tell you how much he hated the surprise party his ex-wife gave him. Believe what you're told.

Suppose you enjoy buying presents and celebrating special occasions, but your date is phobic about both. Don't give up what gives you pleasure. Prepare a small token gift such as a home baked item, a CD, or a bouquet of fall leaves. Say something like: "I know you don't want a fuss made about your birthday but I want you to know I did remember it." And that's all. Don't expect more than brief thanks in return. You've shown you can give something small, without expecting an effusive response. The next holiday might be different for both of you.

- Don't overdo. Less is more. Give gifts that are symbolic. Don't embarrass someone with an item they may not want or need or be able to return because it is too extravagant or intimate.

- Never give a gift that once belonged to a former spouse or partner. Save the string of genuine pearls for your granddaughter. Your new beau doesn't want your dead husband's shop tools, either.
- Homemade offerings are super. But don't give anything shabby. She might not be impressed by the handcrafted bird house and you'll be embarrassed if you don't see it hanging from the eaves the next time you visit. Before you embark on a project, think carefully about the quality. If you're going to knit or sew, get the size right in advance. If you're going to prepare a food item, make sure it's something the recipient enjoys. Don't make assumptions: I know it's hard to believe but I have a female friend who doesn't like chocolate. Her freezer contained a bouquet of chocolate roses for months after last Valentine's Day. (She finally got the nerve to throw them out.)
- Think about enlarging a picture you've taken on a shared activity and put it in a nice frame. Don't blow it up to poster size or expect to see it displayed in the front hall with all the ancestors. A nice four by six or five by seven photo in a simple frame is great.

- Safe bets: CD's; books if you're sure they will be read; jewelry that doesn't imply commitment such as a pin, earrings or a tie tack; tickets to an event; a magazine subscription. Sweaters, scarves, and mufflers are fine when you're dating; postpone giving other clothing items until you are in a committed and intimate relationship. Keep it simple, make or buy a nice card, wrap it nicely, and you've got a winner.

Intimacy

Many people confuse intimacy with self-revelation. But the road to intimacy is a journey you share. You become closer by having experiences together rather than by hearing about what the other person has done before you met them.

Intimacy is defined differently by every person. For one couple, intimacy might involve spending Saturday nights together and nothing else. For another couple, intimacy means sharing every moment and every thought. Assess how much intimacy you can tolerate and what you can accept. Your needs may be very different from your companion's.

Don't push

Think about the difference between dating and courtship. It's subtle but it's there. While dating, you're exploring the possibility of a relationship. As time goes on, you'll decide if this is the person with whom you want to share your future. Trust develops as you come to rely upon each other.

If you're afraid to reveal yourself, because you fear you'll be rejected if someone gets to know you, you can actually prevent intimacy from developing. You must allow yourself to be vulnerable if you want an intimate relationship. Don't assume, however, that your partner is incapable of intimacy just because they haven't opened up and shared their deepest secrets after three months or six months of dating.

Intimacy develops slowly over a period of time. As Rachelle Zukerman wisely advises in *Young at Heart,* as a couple accumulates a shared history, their closeness grows. Shared activities help build a common history and a library of humor and shared moments.

Many men and women experience a sense of urgency as they age, which makes them more likely to rush into a relationship, fearing they'll never get another chance. But they may just be rushing into misery. Take time. Find out if this person is someone you can truly care about and someone who can truly care for you.

What if there is a mismatch in the amount of intimacy you both want? Think about what is offered. Can you live with it? You can share your hobbies or intellectual interests with your good friends. Maybe he doesn't like to dance, but it's fine with him if you dance with others. Do you have enough going on in your life so you don't need a relationship to supply all your needs? The relationship might not be perfect, but no relationship is.

Are we a couple yet?

At some point, you're ready to move forward. You are done with dating, you're ready for a commitment. The word "commitment" covers a lot of possibilities, from reserving Saturday night for a steady movie date to the promise to never look at another. Commitment is a statement, either spoken or implied, that your intention is to make the relationship work. It's an active rather than a passive stance. Because you are invested in this relationship, you're willing to work through problems and find a mutually satisfactory solution.

This transition cannot be rushed. Pushing for promises, when the person you're dating is reluctant or unsure, is a recipe for disaster. A relationship has to evolve at a speed that causes the least discomfort to the person going the slowest. All you can do is communicate your readiness and find out how your date feels. Don't ask for more than your partner can give. There's no benefit to having a relationship with someone who was forced into it by ultimatums or threats. You both want to be ready and willing to make a commitment.

⤛ 8 ⤜

To Bed or Not to Bed?

Gloria and Emory are on their second date, at an intimate Italian restaurant. It's crowded and dark. They are squeezed into a tiny booth for two in the corner. A candle flickers on the table. Over several glasses of Chianti and a delicious meal, they've had a lively conversation about all the places they've lived and where they've traveled. But they're both starting to wonder what's going to happen next.

Emory notices that Gloria brushed his arm as she reached for her water glass. He wonders if that was an accident or — oh no! — a signal that she wants to sleep with him tonight. He's worried about his performance; his last sexual encounter was a disaster.

Gloria is concerned too. She's attracted to Emory but doesn't feel comfortable getting more intimate on a second date. Yet she thinks that if she turns him down, he'll never ask her out again.

Sex after 50

For many centuries, our culture has perpetuated the idea that older people don't have sex. Thankfully, times are changing and this stereotype is gradually being dispelled. People of every generation are more at ease with notions of sensuality.

A survey conducted by the National Council on Aging shows that nearly half of all Americans age sixty or older engage in sexual activity at least once a month. In the same survey of 1,300 people, both men and women said they were pleased with sex and wanted more of it. Half of those interviewed said sex was as good or better as it was when they were younger. Even more reported that sex brought them equal or greater emotional satisfaction than it did when they were in their forties. True, as the decades progress, the general level of activity decreases although men continue to be more active than women. Yet this study revealed that one-third of women in their seventies were sexually active.

The American Association of Retired Persons conducted a survey in 1999 to determine the sexual habits and preferences of older people. Researchers concluded that about half of those interviewed thought that a satisfying sexual relationship was an important element of the good life. Half of those surveyed engaged in sex. They learned that as time passes older people increasingly view their partners as romantic and physically attractive. The researchers also found that taboos about sex outside of marriage were diminishing in this population.

Sex changes with aging, as does so much else in life. The prospect of sex at any age can be daunting, but starting a new sexual relationship after the age of fifty is truly scary. If you haven't had sex for a while, you may wonder if everything still works. Disappointments and disasters from the past may surface. And worst of all, is the realization that at some point you will have to take off your clothes. Will your lover accept and appreciate your aging body?

Women are especially vulnerable to fears about appearance. It's difficult to feel desirable when the world says you're not. Men are considered sexy, even as they age, but older women are usually ignored, both by the media and when walking down the street. The exception is the glamorous movie star, but many of these women are attractive because they look younger than their age.

Still, Joel Block in *Sex Over 50* points out that "Around fifty, men tend to become more emotional about lovemaking, and they start seeking the closeness and intimacy they may have disdained in their youth." Although a man may still fantasize about having sex with a gorgeous, younger woman, he's more likely to be interested in a woman who offers companionship and affection.

Research shows that older men focus less on the physical aspects of a relationship and more on the social and emotional perspective. Men become better at romantic relationships, friendships, and social relationships, while women tend to become more assertive as they grow older. The end result is that men and women become more like each other as they age.

What is sex?

Sex means different things to different people. It can be an affectionate glance, hand-holding, cuddling, petting, or intercourse. Sexual activity preferences can run the gamut from vanilla to kinky.

Many people employ the euphemism "sleeping together" to indicate sex but you actually don't have to sleep together, even after intercourse. In Europe, it is common for couples to get together for sex but sleep in different rooms. This may be more comfortable for someone who is used to sleeping alone. But a partner might be offended, believing the intimacy of sharing a bed is part of the pleasure of sex.

The point is that you have your definition of sex and your partner probably has another. This is one good reason it's important to postpone sexual activity until you've had a chance to discuss your proclivities and restrictions. And again, talking about these topics is not appropriate on a first date.

I suggest the following guidelines:

- No sex on the first date — this is a chance to assess mutual interest, but way too soon to share anything this personal.
- No sex until you've shared medical history relating to sex — this is important information to have, both for your physical and emotional safety. Since it is intimate and often difficult to disclose, you should postpone this conversation until you're certain you want to move ahead with this person.

- No sex until you know your partner is truly committed to being with you and is not involved with other relationships. Again, this requires trust which can only develop over time.

There are, of course, exceptions to these rules — you may not mind if your partner has sex with others. The important thing is to figure out what makes you comfortable. Then you can relax and enjoy the process, knowing what steps you will take towards sexual intimacy.

Sexual chemistry

Let's suppose you've decided you're interested in having sex with your current partner. First you need to be sure the other person is ready. You don't want to have your romantic intimations received with a gasp of horror or a wide-eyed stare. Since you may have been out of the romance business for decades, it's time to brush up on some social cues.

Bring sex into the conversation as a way of putting the issue on the table. Tell an anecdote about how some people you know became lovers. Talk about an aunt and uncle who went on a second honeymoon in their seventies. You get the idea.

Notice casual physical contact. She brushes your hand as she reaches for the water pitcher. He takes your arm while crossing the street. It may be an invitation or simply a friendly gesture. Since everyone has a different social style, you'll have to determine what it means. My advice is to err on the side of caution and bide your time until the future of your relationship is clear. Be sure you have a sense of your companion's boundaries before crossing into uncharted territory.

Can the woman take the initiative? Suppose your guy is being reserved and you're impatient to get things going. This is the twenty-first century and possibilities have expanded. Women are more at ease with kick-starting romance. But know your man. If he is old-fashioned in attitude, or afraid of being pressured, he might be offended or scared off by your advances. Only you can decide if the risk of rejection is worth the gamble.

As Robert N. Butler says in his book *The New Love and Sex After 60*, "An enduring partnership is based on thoughtfulness as well as attraction."

Discussing sex

Once you've determined both of you are interested, you'll want to learn something about each other's sexual history and any health issues related to sex. This can be an awkward conversation and one fraught with anxiety. Plan to talk about this early on, before you're swept away by a romantic moment.

It's best to have this conversation in a neutral setting at a neutral hour. This is not the time for candles and wine. Try for coffee in a café where you can have privacy in late afternoon or early evening.

Start by saying, "Could we talk about sex? I know this isn't easy, but I feel this is really important. What do you think?" You might get an answer such as, "Sorry. This isn't a subject I like to talk about." You can respond: "Well, okay. But there are some things I would like you to know. You don't have to say anything, but would it be all right if I say what's on my mind?"

This approach might help take the pressure off the other person. If this works, keep what you say to a minimum, for instance, "I need to know if there are any medical issues we should discuss. I want sex to be as healthy as possible for both of us." This indicates that safe sex is the topic. Or if you have issues you want to discuss you might say: "There are some things I'd like you to know about." If talking seems uncomfortable, you could suggest alternatives. "I understand it's hard to talk about this subject, but I feel we need to share some information. Want to e-mail? Can we write? What about the phone?"

Rules for sex

There are no absolute rules for sexual behavior. You decide how you want to proceed. Are you willing to bend your own rules? Or will you rely on your lifetime of experience?

It may be time to try something new. Let's say your rule has always been to hold off sex until you feel you're ready. While you believe people get to know each other best by talking and sharing activities, your date believes people get to know each other best by being in bed together. Maybe you'll decide to play by your date's rules and see what happens.

What if you're looking for sex without romance? Be honest with yourself and your partner. For instance, you might say "I've al-

270

ways had problems making a commitment. I really like you, but I'm pretty sure my future won't be any different. Still I enjoy sex, even if it's only for one time. Would you want to spend the night with me anyway?"

What if you're interested in romance but not sex? Maybe you were never very interested in sex. Or sex was a source of conflict in a past relationship — perhaps it was used as a weapon or as a reward. Not everyone wants to be sexually active. You can live a happy and satisfying celibate life and many older people do.

It's vital to know where you stand and express your current wishes. Don't feel inadequate or guilty if you are looking for a relationship where sex does not play a central role. Many relationships in the second half of life are based on mutual interests, affection, and companionship. You may be fulfilled with an arm around the shoulder. Or an admiring glance may be enough to gratify your craving for romance. Sexuality has its nuances and all are acceptable.

Safe sex

It seems easy to avoid the issue of unsafe sex, but the consequences are unpleasant at best and life threatening at worst. Older adults are not immune to sexually transmitted diseases. Viruses and bacteria do not discriminate by age.

AIDS: The most frightening risk to the older population is AIDS. At this writing, according to the U.S. Center for Disease Control and Prevention, AIDS is spreading rapidly among non-gays fifty and older. Of all reported AIDS cases in the US, thirteen percent are found in this age group. The problem is especially dire, since over-fifty heterosexuals are less likely to get tested.

Naiveté, more liberal sexual behavior, and longer lives have combined to create this dangerous situation. According to a recent study, the greatest risk factor for both men and women over fifty is sex with multiple partners. Too many disregard the hazards of unprotected sex. And men in this age group are less likely to use condoms.

Who would suspect a dainty grandma or a happily married CEO could be infected with HIV? But that elegant widow might have received a contaminated blood transfusion before HIV screening started in March 1985. And the CEO was monogamous, except for that one time at a convention when he had too much to drink and went to bed with a woman he met at the bar.

Fiona thought Martin, a wealthy and successful lawyer who traveled around the country giving workshops, was the answer to her dreams. During the year they dated, she noticed he was often sick, he had skin problems, took a lot of pills, and was in the hospital a few times with lung problems, but she thought that was normal in a man of 72. Then Fiona got sick and her family doctor suggested an AIDS test. She was sure it would come up negative. But it didn't. She is still recovering emotionally and physically from the shock of finding out that Martin infected her with HIV.

Herpes: No one is exempt from herpes. The incidence is increasing to epidemic levels in all age groups. By the time they reach 50, most men and women have probably been exposed to it. Use condoms until you know your partner's status and avoid intercourse during an outbreak.

Chlamydia: Less common in older people, Chlamydia can cause painful urination in men and frequent urination and painful intercourse in women. This condition is easily treated with antibiotics.

Hepatitis B: The only sexually transmitted disease that can be prevented by vaccine is Hepatitis B. Any sexually active person, no matter what age, should be vaccinated unless a physician advises against it.

HPV: Human Papilloma Virus is the most common STD in people over fifty. Unfortunately, this illness cannot be prevented. The virus can be transmitted even through a condom. Since it is linked with precancerous lesions on the cervix, women with new sexual partners should get routine pap smears. Genital warts, caused by the same virus are less common, but just as contagious and equally distressing.

Other sexually transmitted diseases: Although increasingly rare, gonorrhea and syphilis still crop up.

It's difficult to ask about your partner's sexual background. But to stay safe you must ask questions pertaining to sexual history:

- Have you had unprotected sex in the past?
- Do you have any of the risk factors for HIV? (Intravenous drug use, blood transfusions, multiple partners, activity with a sexual partner in a high-risk category)
- Have men had male as well as female partners?

- Are you willing to go to your doctor and be tested if I do the same?

You don't know the sexual history of the person you are dating until you ask. And even then there are no guarantees you'll hear the truth. Don't be naïve. Just because you don't have to worry about pregnancy doesn't mean you're safe from other consequences of unprotected sex. If you want more information, ask your doctor. Use condoms. Get tested. Wait until you've gathered sufficient information. Stay safe and live to enjoy your relationship.

Sexual seduction

Sex too soon can extinguish a relationship before it sees the light of day. Sexual fireworks are great. But counting on a night in bed to cement the future is a bad bet. Yes, some couples find their relationship deepens once they become sexual. But sex can also hurry the end with startling and unexpected abruptness.

There can be lots of reasons: the timing is wrong or the couple just isn't right for each other. The intimate act puts a mismatch in glaring perspective. Take it slowly. You're exploring the possibility of something you want to last a long time. You need time to adjust to each other's interests, habits, and quirks. You need to learn each other's sexual agendas.

It can be difficult to turn down an invitation to sex, especially if you like the other person and want to continue seeing them. You might try a statement like this: "I find you attractive and would like to keep dating, but the sexual part of my life is on hold for now."

Saying "later," is a valid response. You may be recovering from an illness, a bad relationship, or the loss of a good one. Make it clear you're interested but want to wait. Your date should respect your wishes. If instead you're being pressured, say good-bye and look for someone who is more in tune with your temperament.

What if the opposite is true? Suppose you're the one initiating sex and your overture is rebuffed? Or even worse, your partner declines to see you again after one sexual encounter? It feels terrible but if it's any consolation, it probably has nothing to do with you. After all, the other person is an adult with half a century of baggage about sexuality. If you know your partner's expectations before the first time, you'll avoid surprise and disappointment.

What if you're swept away by the heat of passion? Maybe you spent the night although you intended to leave. Now you feel awful but you don't know how the other person feels. Call. Ask to get together in a neutral setting. Say you'd like to talk about what happened. Have your discussion in person and not on the phone or by e-mail. "I really want to get to know you, but things happened so fast. I would like to have a romantic relationship with you, but this is too soon. What do you think?"

No matter how experienced you are, you can make mistakes. Short of having unprotected sex or putting yourself in a physically unsafe situation, none are fatal, just embarrassing. As long as you're alive, you have the chance to forgive yourself for blunders and try again.

You can agonize about the decision to begin a sexual relationship for weeks or the transition can occur with such speed that you hardly realize it has happened. Since each relationship is unique, the timing will be different too. Move slowly and carefully. Premature intimacy can push your connection off course and make it difficult, if not impossible, to get back on track. On the other hand, once you've introduced sex into your connection, you add complexity, commitment, and pleasure to your relationship.

The first time

The first time you have sex with a new partner is a special occasion. It can be disappointing, funny (maybe only in retrospect) or blissful. To maximize your chances of pleasure, consider the best possible circumstances.

Decide whether you'll be most at ease in a morning or afternoon. Not everyone enjoys sex at night.

Choose a suitable setting. You want maximum comfort, minimal pressure and privacy. A night at a fancy hotel might be intimidating. Perhaps you'd prefer a local bed-and-breakfast.

Worried about how you look without clothes? When someone looks at you with love and desire, they may not notice the things you consider flaws. Beauty is truly in the eye of the beholder. If you know where you're going for that first romantic night, provide low lights. Have candles and soft music. Both men and women look better in attractive underwear. Keep a robe handy to put on after you make love.

Be sure the setting is clean, orderly, and private. If you are planning to invite someone home, make sure no children or grandchildren are nearby. Candles are romantic; pill bottles are not. Put your medical equipment in the closet, your antifungal creams in the medicine cabinet, your dirty underwear in the laundry basket. You might also want to remove personal pictures and reminders of previous lovers. Ghosts in the room can squash the libido.

Susan loved Roger, but she had a hard time staying over at his house. Roger was a widower — his wife had died two years before he met Susan — but he had never put away his wife's personal items. Her necklaces and earrings were still displayed on a rack above the dresser. Every time Susan opened the closet she saw the wife's size-five heels, which make her self-conscious about her big feet. She was reluctant to ask Roger to remove these items, feeling that they must be meaningful to him, yet she always felt like she was an understudy in his bedroom.

Sex: fact and fiction

First, the facts:

- People who have been sexually active usually remain active. Sex may be less intense or less frequent, but it is still satisfying. The medical explanation is testosterone. This is the primary hormonal force behind both male and female sex drives. A third of menopausal women have decreased sex drives because of lower levels of testosterone. For men, testosterone concentration in the blood declines, lowering interest and drive. But bear in mind: testosterone is reduced but not gone.
- Sex is good for you. It burns calories, keeps muscles working, and boosts the body's immune system. Sex qualifies as exercise and like any exercise, the more you do it, the better you get. Women who have sex regularly report less problems with mild urinary incontinence. Older people who have sex regularly have better self-esteem, body image, and emotional well-being than those who are celibate.
- Sex improves with age. Fear of pregnancy is gone. A deepening sexual relationship with one person often replaces the desire

for multiple conquests. True intimacy can make it easier to share fantasies and try new possibilities.

Now for some fiction:

- Losing desire is a natural and inevitable part of aging. Diminish? Maybe. Lose? Never!
- Bad for the heart. The American Heart Association says: No problem. "There's no reason why a heart patient or a stroke survivor can't resume usual sexual activity as soon as they feel ready."
- The penis shrinks with age. Stop worrying and throw away your tape measure.
- No more orgasms. No way! A healthy woman's frequency of orgasm can increase with each decade until her eighties. For men, there may be less semen, less forceful ejaculations, and more time needed between erections, but the end result is still enjoyable.
- Women lose interest in sex after menopause. Women's interest in sex often increases. The fear of unwanted pregnancy is gone and children have grown and left the home. This is a time for new activities and interests. "One of the best-kept secrets is

how intrinsically sexy older women are," say Avis and Gina Ogden in *Women Who Love Sex*. "Women have the physical capacity to sustain sexuality in the later years. Many women might rediscover their passion or even find it for the first time if they believed they could overcome the roadblocks that keep them from making a rich sex life into old age a reality."

Solving sexual problems

"I just can't imagine a relationship without sex," said Matt, a handsome, silver-haired man of sixty-six. He had come to see me, along with his girlfriend, Ginny, to discuss a sexual performance problem. "It's always been a part of my life — I've had two wives and plenty of girlfriends. I've always thought sex would be as natural as breathing. But now . . ." He broke off and looked over at Ginny. She gave him an encouraging smile. "We've been together for six months and I think I'd like to make it permanent. Only there's no sex. It's not that she doesn't want it. I try and it doesn't work. Ginny is patient, but I'm not sure how much longer she'll put up with this. And I don't know how much longer I want to keep trying. It's so embarrassing."

I asked Matt a few questions to establish if there were any underlying physical factors that could be affecting his performance. But he was not depressed. In fact he said he felt better than ever. He did have high blood pressure but he was taking medication to control it, eating well, and working out at the gym three times a week.

Ginny, a trim sixty-year-old administrator, sat listening patiently while Matt described his problem. "I do like sex," she said, "but I'm willing to wait until things are right again."

I ended up working with Matt and Ginny in couple's counseling for several months. It turned out that impotence was a side effect of the blood pressure medication Mark was taking. But there were other issues as well. Matt's anxiety about not being able to perform made his chance of success slim. And Matt was making a big change. A ladies man for years, he had always chosen previous partners based on appearance and chemistry, but he had chosen Ginny for affection and companionship. And Ginny was almost "too understanding." This made him feel guilty — not a good scenario for a happy sex life.

Viagra and Its Cousins

Erectile dysfunction affects more than 30 million men in the United States, more than 150 million men worldwide, and accounts for half a million visits to health care providers annually. In 1998 Viagra (sildenafil citrate) took the country by storm, giving new opportunity to men who had thought that their sexual life was over. In 2003, two new pills for the treatment of erectile dysfunction became available in Europe and in the United States. They are Levitra (vardenafil HCI), developed by the Bayer Corporation; and Cialis (tadalafil), developed by Lilly.

These three work by the same mechanism: they inhibit phosphodiesterase, a chemical naturally produced by the body. When this enzyme is blocked, the penis' smooth muscles relax and permit blood flow to increase. With sufficient inflow of blood, the penis becomes erect.

These drugs behave in similar ways. They don't produce an erection on their own but require sexual stimulation for response. Eighty percent of men trying these medicines report erections sufficiently improved to permit successful intercourse. There are no published studies yet comparing the drugs to each other. Men may do well with one medicine while finding another ineffective. Possible side effects are the same: headache, facial flushing, running nose, changes in vision and stomach distress. While muscle aches and back pain can occur with all three drugs, these complaints seem to be more common with Cialis. The cause of this is not clear. The response to Viagra is slower following a high-fat meal but Levitra and Cialis aren't influenced by food or alcohol.

Viagra begins to work within 30 minutes of being ingested and the effects last about four hours. Cialis starts to work in 15 to 30 minutes. Its effects can last as long as 36 hours. Levitra is taken an hour before planned sexual activity and lasts about 4 hours.

Before taking any of these, check with your doctor if you have heart disease or are taking heart medicines. See a doctor if your erection lasts longer than 4 hours because this can cause permanent damage to the penis.

New medications such as apomorphine taken by placing it under the tongue or as a nasal spray and Topigaln (alprostadil) gel or Alprox-TD (alprostadil) cream for topical use are in the wings. They may not be far behind in the successful treatment of a problem that concerns millions of men and their partners.

After several counseling sessions and a trip to his doctor, Matt found he could function quite well. Changing the blood pressure medication helped. Matt also got in touch with his feelings about aging and accepted that although he might not have chosen Ginny in his younger days, she was the woman he wanted to marry.

Think about what you might do to enhance desire before a relationship begins. Educating yourself in advance lessens anxiety. Be proactive rather than waiting until problems occur and then scrambling for solutions. As you look for explanations to your difficulties, be wary of what you read or hear. View material with a critical eye. Watch out for the words "never" and "always." The answers to your questions seldom lie in one area alone, whether it is hormonal imbalance, psychological issue, or medical explanation.

If you're planning to date and know your sexual performance isn't right, visit your doctor. Provide a complete picture of your sexual history. Be honest about smoking, drinking, and your current over-the-counter medications. Your doctor might prescribe drugs that enhance sexual drive and function. Try masturbation to see if these are working.

Many drugs dampen interest in sex and make it hard to function. If you research the side effects of your medicines on the web, you may be overwhelmed. It's hard to recognize helpful, accurate information in the sea of opinions and personal anecdotes. If you want to use the web, check out legitimate sites such as <u>merckmedicus.com</u>. Select "Patient resources" then choose "Best practice of medicine–Patient guide." Or try <u>healthsquare.com</u> and select "drugs and medicines" for a comprehensive list of side effects from the authoritative Physician's Desk Reference.

There are even safer strategies than relying on the Internet. Discuss your medicines with your physician or pharmacist. These professionals have ready access to clear, correct information about benefits and side effects. To be most helpful, make them aware of your complete list of drugs. Approximately two hundred medicines have sexual side effects. If you are taking one of these and your doctor cannot suggest an alternative, ask about trying the medicine in a slightly lower dose. Sometimes this strategy provides efficacy and eliminates the sexually inhibiting consequences.

Below is a list of commonly prescribed problem medicines:

- Antidepressants. The Selective Serotonin Reuptake Inhibitors (SSRI's), the most popular class of antidepressants, including Prozac, Zoloft, and Paxil, can delay or prevent ejaculation in men and reduce desire and orgasm in women. Sometimes it's hard to tell if sexual difficulties are caused by the depression the medications are meant to treat or by the treatment itself. Ask your doctor about alternatives such as Welbutrin.
- Antihypertensives for high blood pressure.
- Steroids for arthritis and other conditions.

Other culprits include alcohol, tobacco, and illegal drugs; these substances may reduce inhibition, but simultaneously reduce ability to function. Stress and fatigue can also diminish sexual performance. As does the exhaustion and psychological trauma of serious illness.

Aging itself does not cause sexual problems. Don't believe you have to give up sex because you're getting older. You are entitled to a rich and satisfying sex life.

Sex after 50 for women

A woman's state of physical and emotional health has a far greater effect on sexual behavior than menopause. Still there are certain conditions associated with menopause that may affect sexual functioning in women. Vaginal dryness, hot flashes, and insomnia can be problematic. When treated, these symptoms diminish, often improving general well-being and increasing interest in sex.

Advertising preys upon women's yearning to treat symptoms. Avoid medication, such as the "natural" concoctions offered on TV and over the Internet. Sellers hawk their merchandise with blatantly false claims. Products such as "Wild Yam Cream" claim to increase libido as well as address a multitude of troubles like "foggy thinking." Many herbals do contain small amounts of hormones which may or may not be helpful. Because these compounds aren't regulated, there is no telling how much hormone they contain. See your doctor; save your money.

Vaginal dryness: Insufficient estrogen decreases vaginal lubrication. A woman and her partner may equate dryness with lack of interest. Proceeding with intercourse can be painful. Hormone creams such as Premarin can be applied directly intravaginally so it isn't absorbed into the body. Because dry areas include the urinary tract, menopausal women are prone to infection. If you plan to have sex, keep an over-the-counter water-based lubricant at hand. Don't use petroleum-based lubricants such as Vaseline. They weaken latex condoms and cause vaginal infections. Avoid lubricants containing perfumes as these can cause skin allergy and irritation. Astro-glide or K-Y Jelly, which can be purchased in the pharmacy, work well.

Low libido: Will a pill help restore lost libido? Do aging women lack blood flow to their genital organs? The answers aren't known yet. Despite anecdotal reports of success, medical studies show that women taking Viagra receive no more benefit than those taking a placebo. Unfortunately, scientists are still in the early stages of research on brain chemicals that activate during sexual response. There isn't a pill yet but Decision Resource, a Massachusetts consulting company, predicts women will spend $1.7 billion dollars by 2008 for libido-enhancing products.

For unresponsive women, testosterone replacement gives a fifty percent rate of improvement. As of the writing of this book, the FDA doesn't yet recognize testosterone deficiency in women, so it's considered a "vanity" medicine — making approval of such drugs problematic. Pure testosterone is marketed for men in dosages too high for women. Although controversial, some gynecologists offer patients a small dose to increase libido either by itself or combined with estrogen, e.g., Estratest tablets. Success is questionable and there are unpleasant side effects: hair loss, weight gain, and hoarseness even in smaller doses.

One alternative is DHEA, a steroid hormone produced by the adrenal gland, which is converted by the body into estrogen and testosterone. Results with this drug have been mixed.

Your doctor is the best source of information on whether you should use hormone replacement therapy, such as a pill, patch, or cream.

Sex after 50 for men

It's important to differentiate between performance and intimacy. Sexuality is traditionally defined in terms of the ability to have an erection and the frequency of intercourse. The focus on erection and coitus actually limits the expression of male sexuality. Remember that talk, fantasy, masturbation, and touching all fit into the mix.

Aging does affect male sexual response. The hardness and duration of the erection diminish due to changes in the tissue structure of the penis and its blood flow. Although orgasm is less frequent, many men get erections into their seventies and eighties. Premature ejaculation becomes less of an issue. The urge for sexual gratification may decrease with age, but the sexual act is just as satisfying.

Impotence: In the AARP 1999 study, twenty-five percent of men interviewed acknowledged being completely or moderately impotent. Yet only half of this group sought help for the problem. In all, there are an estimated thirty million men with total or partial impotence. The good news is that there are treatments available. The bad news is that so few men seek treatment.

Aging is not necessarily the problem. Erectile dysfunction is often caused by a mixture of problems. There can be psychological causes, social issues, or medical reasons. A specialist in male sexual dysfunction or urologist can help.

Viagra and similar medications improve erectile dysfunction for about seventy to eighty percent of patients. Urologists have machines, injections, and surgery for improving blood supply to the genital area. As a last resort, an implant can be placed in the penis to make it firm while engaging in sex. A specialist in erectile dysfunction says, "Most men can be treated."

Be wary of herbal sex enhancers, advertised on TV and radio as "Viagra alternatives." Most of these boost nothing but the profit margins of the companies that make them. Yohimbine, originating from an African tree has been prescribed for years and is said to be twenty-five percent more effective than a placebo. But it sometimes causes nausea and drowsiness which would certainly dampen the desire for sex.

Since there is no government oversight of herbal supplements, there are no guarantees. The listed ingredients may not be accurate; supplements can contain toxins or heavy metals. If advertisers imply they can cure impotence, the FDA or FTC can nail them for false claims or bogus advertising. So advertisers use vague and non-committal phrases such as "improving function and performance." These terms could just as well apply to skill with the violin. Do herbal supplements work? Maybe, for some. Remember the placebo factor, if you believe it's going to work it may work for you.

Psychological factors

The most common cause of sexual dysfunction is fear of intimacy and rejection. Both men and women worry about performance. Some people are afraid their sexual desires are weird or abnormal. Others are afraid they will be judged inadequate.

People who fear intimacy sometimes protect themselves emotionally. They look for excuses to reject partners so they need not have sex. Or they use sex to keep partners at a distance. Sex feels close but can be a way of avoiding real emotional intimacy. People with difficulty with true attachment can tolerate transient physical closeness but often pull back when the objects of their affection return their interest.

The capacity for intimacy is rooted in childhood events. It can be developed at later stages in life, but only with effort. When beginning to date, do not expect a person will change. Try to find out his or her historical pattern and determine if it's acceptable to you.

Whenever you start a relationship, you face the possibility of rejection. There is no guarantee you're going to be a match with the other person. Protect yourself by realizing that dating is a process of exploration. Either person has the right to call a halt at any time. Butler says it beautifully: "Rejection is nature's way of keeping two people apart who should not be together."

Both men and women have concerns about being physically attractive. We want to see ourselves and be seen by others as sexy. But as we grow older that becomes more difficult, since our society places such a premium on youthful beauty. You can't change society, but you cultivate an image of yourself as warm, sexy, and friendly. If you project this attitude, others will believe you. All of this will be much less of a problem if you and your date get to like each other — before sex.

For many people who are having sex for the first time with a new partner, the major stumbling block is the fear of being naked. You can make love without removing all your clothes. Women can wear a sexy slip. Men can leave on any undergarments that might help.

Will losing weight improve your libido? Yes, feeling slimmer can make you feel sexier. Does being overweight mean you can't feel sexy? Absolutely not. Some men and women enjoy sex with larger people. The answer lies in finding the right partner.

Emotional heaviness can be even more problematic than physical weight. Depression and anger dull desire. Guilt in any form inhibits successful sex. People can feel guilty about having sexual desire. They may feel disloyal to a previous spouse. Some believe they are betraying their children's trust by having sex.

If you have unresolved issues, maybe sex isn't something you want in a relationship right now. Would some other non-erotic physical contact be acceptable? Consider what you can tolerate and be hopeful that as time passes your level of comfort will change.

Everyone has past relationship baggage. You might have had bad sex, no sex, or sex so good that it would be a hard act to follow. Now is the time to put thoughts of previous lovers on the back burner. Stay in the present. If you can't do this, consider holding off a new sexual connection until these issues get resolved on your own or with the help of a therapist.

Maybe you've been celibate for a long time. You'd like to give sex a try, but you're afraid you've forgotten how. Like so many other things in life, a dress rehearsal is good preparation. Get your juices flowing by thinking about sex. Depending on what you find comfortable, you might read romantic books, look at magazines, fantasize, and masturbate.

Resources

Your doctor is still your best resource. Unfortunately, the average primary care physician has about one minute, if that much, to answer the questions of a patient who comes with sexual concerns. But it's still a good place to start. Doctors are becoming more aware of the emotional needs of patients and learning not to ignore concerns about older people and sex. Your doctor may refer you to a gynecologist, urologist, or counselor who has the time and expertise you need.

A variety of experts can advise about sexual matters. Find someone with whom you're comfortable. Clergy, social workers, psychotherapists, and psychiatrists address the questions of both the heterosexual and homosexual community. Even before you're a committed couple, you can consult a couples' therapist for advice on sex.

Sex is often a delicate issue, but a call to the psychiatry department of your local medical school will result in names of specialists, such as urologists, who can help. If you're shy about talking about sex issues, write your questions down before your consultation. You may feel more comfortable reading from a list and taking notes on the answers. And you're less likely to forget an important concern.

Gloria and Emory's second date did not have a happy ending. Thinking Gloria expected him to make an advance, Emory asked her if she wanted to stop at his place for coffee. Since Gloria believed if she refused, Emory wouldn't see her again, she agreed reluctantly. Once they were settled on his sofa with their cups of coffee, Emory put his arms around her and began kissing her. But Gloria could sense his approach lacked a certain enthusiasm. She figured it was because she was overweight. She struggled out of his embrace, grabbed her coat and told him she wanted to go home.

Gloria didn't expect Emory to call again. To her surprise, he did but it took him three weeks to get up the courage. At first he felt insulted by Gloria's abrupt rejection, but later he realized he didn't feel comfortable either. Besides he liked her — she was good-natured and, to be honest, she had offered to share the cost of dinner, something neither of his ex-wives had ever done.

Gloria and Emory began dating again, but moving slowly. Their dates ended with a hug and a promise to call. After three months, Emory suggested a weekend away together. He made reservations at a mountain lodge and packed a bottle of champagne. Gloria brought a nightgown and a scented candle.

By the time the weekend came around they were both ready. They'd had the chance to talk about how they felt and what they wanted. They spoke about their fears. To her relief, Gloria learned that Emory was totally unconcerned about her weight. He thought she looked great. Gloria was financially independent and quite comfortable so Emory knew she appreciated him, not his bankbook. With all this behind them, sex was better than ever!

❖ 9 ❖

Making the Most of It

This chapter is about the process of becoming a couple and takes you up to the time when you're in a committed relationship whether it's marriage, living together, or a less traditional arrangement. This exploratory phase of the relationship can last months or years.

Remain flexible

By the time you've passed 50, you have certain standards. Your preferences are set. Everyone assumes that flexibility isn't a quality that's enhanced with age. But I encourage you to test your limits. See if you can live with qualities you previously thought difficult. Take, for example, crabbiness. An irritable person can still be reliable, honest, empathic, and kind. Some qualities are nonnegotiable, like trust and safety. But do think about areas where you can cut your date some slack.

Instead of searching for your perfect partner, your true love, your one and only soulmate, look for someone you enjoy, with whom you can plan and share a future. A "good enough" relationship can give a great deal of pleasure.

You might have to give something up but perhaps it will be worth it. Heidi gave up eating at expensive restaurants because Ben was on a much tighter budget than she was. They compromised by splurging on one fancy dinner a month; meanwhile Ben polished his skills as a low-budget gourmet chef, whipping up fabulous meals for the two of them.

Maybe you'll be inspired to adopt new hobbies or learn new skills. I was not the slightest bit interested in rock climbing until my boyfriend, an avid climber, suggested I learn. It wasn't as scary as I feared and now it's one of my favorite recreational activities.

Little white lies

Catching your date in a fabrication can also cause trouble. If it's the first time, be sympathetic. Try to understand why your companion resorted to an invention. Can you get past the issue?

If you can forgive and move on, that's fine. If you're going to carry anger and hurt like a weight on your shoulders, it is time to end the relationship.

Asking for change

As you get to know your companion, you may encounter behaviors you don't like. Address these issues with respect. Don't nag or shame your partner. After all, you aren't engaged — you're simply exploring the possibility of a relationship. And, at this point, you want to know if your companion is willing to listen to your concerns and make changes.

Pick your issue. Don't dump a whole laundry list of complaints on your date at one time. Just focus on the one that's most important to you.

Pete had a pretty good relationship with Carla. She shared his interests in golf and ballroom dancing, which was important to him. They both enjoyed spending time with their grandchildren and their families liked and accepted them as a couple.

Sure, Pete had some misgivings. He

thought Carla wore her clothes too tight and too short. He also didn't like the way she criticized his golf swing or his waltz steps. But, what really bothered him was the way she made promises she didn't keep. She would say she would get tickets for a show but never mention it again. Once he mentioned how much he loved pumpkin pie and she promised to bake him one, but the pie never materialized.

Pete didn't think he could change Carla but he doubted he could live with this behavior. Wondering if he should or could compromise, Pete started seeing a therapist who helped Pete sort out his priorities. Many of Carla's behaviors bothered him but Pete was most disturbed by broken promises. The therapist suggested Pete talk to Carla the next time she let him down and they rehearsed what Pete might say so he could voice his concerns in a neutral and respectful way.

Pete got an opportunity to practice this new approach when Carla promised to get tickets for a concert. The date came and went without any mention of the concert. The following night, before heading out for dinner, Pete asked Carla to sit down and talk to him.

"Carla," he said, "there's something that

bothers me. You tell me you'll do something, like getting tickets for the concert last night. Since I believe what you say, I expect you to follow through. I know things can change, but I get hurt when I look forward to something and it doesn't happen. I'd rather you surprise me. As long as you don't tell me you're going to do something in advance, I won't be disappointed. What do you think?"

Carla was surprised by Pete's comments. She had never thought much about her behavior. She frequently talked about things she would like to do, without feeling any compunction to follow through. Once she understood how it affected Pete, she tried to restrain this tendency. But even better, because the subject was out in the open, they could laugh at her "promises" and the issue became much less of a problem.

Many relationships dissolve over the issue of broken "promises," I put this word in quotation marks because sometimes the promise is nothing more than a flight of fancy. Suppose on a cold winter night, your companion says, "It would be nice to sell my house and buy a boat. We could cruise the Caribbean for a year." Is this a promise? Or a romantic fantasy?

In the flush of romance, it's easy to make

these statements. You make all sorts of plans — a visit to the museum, a hand-knitted sweater, moving to Costa Rica. One or two of these good-natured wishful musings can be pleasant and harmless — they help you develop a vision of your shared future.

But when your partner keeps making statements like this and doesn't follow through, you may get angry. If the relationship is otherwise good, say something about how this affects you. "I know you mean well when you talk about knitting me a sweater. But when it doesn't happen, I'm disappointed. I'd prefer if you just surprise me. I don't want to look forward to something that might not happen." If the head-in-the-cloud musings continue, it may be time to move on.

Speaking before thinking is another common behavior crying out for change. Maybe your companion doesn't realize it's rude to comment on your weight or point out the deficits in your education. A simple comment like, "You hurt my feelings when you say this," should be enough. It's hard to alter old patterns, so you may have to make this statement more than once. However, if your date continues to make hurtful remarks, despite your comments, you're dating someone mean. What a grim future if you should decide to continue.

Suppose you've accumulated a list of grievances. It's reasonable to address each one as a problem and not as character assassination. "This bothers me." (You acknowledge that this is something you feel and you're not blaming the other person.) "What can we do to make it better?" (You recognize it's a shared problem, and you're willing to work on it too.) "Help me figure this out." (Asking for help indicates you respect your date's opinions and expect a responsible and caring response.) All excellent statements.

Being flexible

In the past, you might have expected someone to meet certain standards, but now you realize what's really important. So what if your date wears white athletic socks with black dress shoes? Suppose this man is kind, considerate, calls when he promises and has a fine family with whom you've just spent a pleasant Christmas. Would you throw away a satisfactory relationship because of a fashion *faux pas?*

Maybe you never dreamed of spending

time with anyone who wasn't able to compete at marathon level. But a slow walk in the park might be just as pleasant if you're with a woman who's funny, compassionate, and willing to bring you soup when you're sick.

You won't be able to let go of all your preferences. I am simply suggesting you give it a try and don't limit your options too soon. Give affection a chance to develop. There's nothing wrong with telling your companion, "I've always dated women who are as athletic as I am. I know you're not. It may be something that will get in the way of our having a long-term relationship. But I'm willing to see how things go and make no promises for the future. What do you think?"

A statement like this is good on several accounts. First, you're not using the phrase, "I have to be honest with you," which implies you were less than honest in the past. Also you're making clear where you stand and most important, you're offering the other person a chance to contribute to the discussion.

Your date might not be willing to take the chance. On the other hand, she might surprise you with a clever compromise or a solution. Maybe she is willing to cheer you on at your Thursday night basketball games or perhaps she'll ask you to teach her to play tennis.

Being flexible is useful. Being overly compliant and accepting behavior you don't like just to maintain the status quo is destructive in the long run.

Alternative arrangements

There are many ways a relationship can work, and this is especially true for older people. We have long personal histories, established family structures, and a pretty clear idea of what we like. We may find the love of a lifetime — the close, committed, and intimate relationship we've always dreamed of. Or we might enjoy a relationship that is less traditional but satisfying nonetheless.

Dating only

Some couples live separately but see each other regularly. You may enjoy the flexibility and independence of this arrangement. Perhaps you want an escort for certain social functions or a romantic interlude once a week. Here, as in all other instances, it's important to clarify the nature of the relationship. Is it okay to date others? Are you both happy with the frequency and duration of time spent together? The key is to remove the mystery and thereby diminish the anxiety.

Minimal dating and companionship

Maybe you've realized you're not in love or you've decided you're never going to live together. But you still enjoy each other's company, with or without sex. Some couples spend time together, either companionable or passionate, for holidays and vacations. This may be all both of you want. Or it may be all one can offer the other. This is a perfectly acceptable option.

Dating a married or otherwise committed person

I don't make any secret of my strong feelings against having a relationship based on deception and exclusion. But such relationships happen. If you decide to enter into such a relationship, be aware of the risks you're taking. At the very best, your relationship will be clouded by deceit and secrets. At the worst, you might put yourself in physical danger. In between, runs a gamut of heartbreak from lonely holidays to destroyed marriages and betrayed friendships. Try to act with as much honesty as the situation allows. Think about why you're doing this. Seek help to explore what you get from this relationship and what unconscious needs you're playing out in the process.

I remember watching such a romance happening in the musty stacks of the University library where I was doing my research. Lucille worked in the Interlibrary Loan division which was located in a tiny cubbyhole in the basement of the library. She was almost always alone, surrounded by stacks of paper, computers, and huge reference books, except when a frantic student arrived to demand immediate access to some obscure text.

Ramon was a book salesman who had been sent down to Lucille's cave and kept returning even though he had never sold her a book. Although he was married, he told Lucille, his relationship with his wife had soured. He was a heavy man, who walked with a bit of a limp and carried a cane since he was almost legally blind.

But despite his unprepossessing appearance, Lucille lit up when he arrived for his monthly sales calls. I could always tell when he was due because Lucille curled her hair, wore makeup and tied a colorful silk scarf around her neck. I wondered if Ramon had given her that scarf as a gift.

I have a thorough distaste for infidelity. But I must confess I had a soft spot for this older couple who seemed to be enjoying their stolen moments of love, without hurting anyone else. I'd watch them go off for long lunches, Ramon offering his arm to Lucille, while she slowed her pace to match his. I never knew how they spent those hours together but I feel better not knowing.

But it was sad watching Lucille waiting for him on this one day when she obviously expected him but he didn't arrive. There she was, all dressed up and wearing her scarf, swiveling her head every time she heard the elevator doors open, but no Ramon. Perhaps he was ill. Or perhaps he died. My project ended and I didn't want to intrude on Lucille's privacy and ask what had happened.

Older/younger combos

We're used to the stereotype of the silver-haired older man with an attractive young woman at his side. Traditionally, women trade youth, fertility, and energy for the older man's financial and emotional protection. But in today's society, roles are fluid and people are flexible. So today it's relatively common for an older woman to find happiness with a younger man.

Karina was 59 when she met Chris, who was 35, in a community college class on cooking. Chris was an unemployed computer programmer who had been laid off and had little prospect of finding another job in the shrinking high-tech industry. Although he had done well in college and graduate school, he had always liked fixing things. So he decided to retrain as an auto mechanic; he was taking the cooking class for elective credits.

Karina had been widowed for two-and-a-half years and was tired of having dinner with couples and going to the movies alone. She went on a few dates with men her age but she didn't find any of them attractive.

Chris noticed that Karina, despite her grey hair and a few wrinkles, was full of life. She was much more dynamic and confident than women his own age. And unlike his previous girlfriend, she had no objection to dating an auto mechanic. Karina wasn't looking for someone to support her financially. She didn't want a husband, just a companion, and a lover.

> *"Instead of searching for your perfect partner, your true love, your one and only soulmate, look for someone you enjoy, with whom you can plan and share a future. A 'good enough' relationship can give a great deal of pleasure."*

Chris was scared at first. "She was so successful and glamorous and incredibly sexy. I was afraid that she would know much more than me."

But they got along well together. Chris thought carefully about what sorts of events Karina would like. She was game to try things she had never tried before. They became devoted fans of a local rock band. And although neither had cared for gardening before, they spent the summer converting Karina's back yard into a huge vegetable patch.

Despite their satisfaction, they did run

into problems. Her friends teased her about "finding a stud." His friends made remarks about how much easier his life was now he was dating a woman with a good income. It was hard to socialize with friends from decidedly different age groups. After a few months of dating, they decided it worked better to see their individual friends separately, although they sometimes got together with one couple who made a special point of never alluding to their ages.

There were also difficult moments when they were out in public. Once a young saleswoman in a department store commented on how nice Chris's "mother" looked in the sweater she was trying on. Karina nearly burst into tears. Chris put his arm around her and said to the young woman, "She's my girlfriend. Grown-ups have enough wisdom to fall in love without paying too much attention to appearances. I hope you're that wise when you grow up!"

Jealousy

My friend, Carolyn, struggles more with jealousy than anyone I've ever known. She's had a long history of bad experiences with men who cheated on her, lied to her or broke up with her when they met someone new. She always believed the other women were prettier, smarter or more successful, even though, in her heart of hearts, she knew this probably wasn't true. Most likely, this pattern began in childhood, since her parents favored her younger sister. But despite years of psychotherapy she just couldn't convert her suspicious nature to one of trust. Jealousy would come over her in giant waves, causing stomachaches, headaches, and wild emotional outbursts.

By the time she was in her 50s, Carolyn gave up on getting rid of her jealousy and decided to find a guy who didn't trigger it. And she thought she had found him in Jim. Jim, who was in his 60s, had a history of failed relationships, probably because of his surliness. But Carolyn was willing to put up with this, since he had many other good points and he definitely wasn't a flirt.

Then, after they had been dating for six months, Jim told her he was throwing a party for an "old friend" who was coming over from Italy on holiday. Anna-Maria was an attractive older woman Jim had met through the Internet. She was barely polite to Carolyn and she monopolized Jim for the week she was in town. Carolyn was immediately consumed with churning doubts. It didn't help that Jim, a man of few words, didn't say anything to reassure her.

Jealousy is an all-consuming envy, resentment, and possessiveness we feel when we think our relationship, our status in life, our friendships, or our possessions are somehow threatened. It's a natural emotion. We become attached to others and to things we see as essential for our well-being and happiness. It's only when this deadly emotion becomes excessive that it causes problems. Ironically, excessive suspicion of a partner, especially if unfounded, is often the very thing that drives the partner away — the exact opposite of what the jealous person wanted to achieve.

Sometimes jealousy comes from the past. Maybe your previous partner cheated, or adultery ripped apart your parents' marriage. Jealousy can arise when you are afraid of a previous painful event repeating itself, especially if you're unable to separate your previous experiences from the current situation.

Insecurity can also be at the root of suspicion. If you feel you don't deserve your partner, you may start looking for signs of desertion. The same thing can happen if you believe the relationship is essential to your well-being. Fear of losing it might cause you to cling too tightly.

Jealousy is a destructive emotion without discernible benefit. It is difficult to have a meaningful relationship with someone who is constantly suspicious of everything you do. It is also miserable to be consumed by fear and uncertainty. Jealousy turns everyday thought into pure self-destructive torture.

What to do if you're plagued by jealousy

- Take stock of yourself. Do you have a history of troubled relationships characterized by dramas and betrayals? If there is a recognizable pattern in your relationships, you might seek professional help so you can make healthier choices in the future.
- If you worry your partner will eventually recognize your shortcomings and find someone better, you might be suffering from a miserable image of yourself. Esteem issues cannot be worked out in a relationship — you have to do it yourself with the help of a therapist.

- If you feel your entire life is dependent on this relationship and the things you do together, you need to cultivate a life of your own. Develop outside interests, rekindle old friendships, and explore new hobbies. Affirm your existence outside of the relationship. If you're too dependent on your partner, you'll make him feel claustrophobic before long.
- Imagine a new life for yourself. Your present partner may not be the right one for you. Maybe you need some time by yourself to sort through issues. You won't die if you lose this person, even though it may feel like that right now.
- Sometimes you know your feelings are unreasonable but you still can't control your jealousy. You may even recognize the destructive nature of indulging in the feelings and the resulting behavior, but you can't stop. It's time to seek professional help.
- While fleeting worries are normal, excessive jealousy is serious. You should be concerned if you become obsessive, constantly imagining ways your partner is betraying you, or if you start checking up on your partner's whereabouts, either by calling constantly or following her to see where she goes and who she's meeting.

This shows not only a lack of trust but a dangerous sense of paranoia on your part. It's time to seek help.

What to do if your partner is the jealous one

Jealousy can make your life a living hell. Get into couples' therapy and see if something can be sorted out. If you feel yourself becoming more isolated, while being watched over by a possessive partner, you might have to plan an exit. Be careful. It is at this point that some jealous people turn dangerous. Don't break the news you're leaving without backup support from family members or friends, especially if there is a history of violence in your relationship.

Even though Anna-Maria was safely back in Italy and unlikely to return to the US for a visit, Carolyn couldn't bear the idea that Jim was continuing his relationship with her over the Internet. She finally told Jim, "I've done everything I can but nothing works. I can't stand knowing you have a relationship with this woman. I know it's baggage from my past but I can't make it go away. As much as I care about you, it's too difficult for me to continue under these circumstances."

Carolyn was delivering an ultimatum, almost always a dangerous thing to do in a relationship but this one worked, perhaps because she was willing to shoulder the responsibility for her feelings instead of blaming Jim. He thought about it, and decided he'd rather have the company of a real live woman rather than continue his e-mail flirtation with Anna-Maria.

Money

In the early stages of dating, you should decide how you want to manage your finances if you decide to make a long term commitment, to a steady romantic partner or by getting married. Determine how much money you need in the future and where that will come from. Think about inheritances and a will and how you can protect your interests if you choose to share your life in the future. Like so many other things, it's best to make these decisions when you're not under any pressure. Decide as much as you can in advance so when tough issues arise, you won't be swayed by the emotions of the moment.

Retirement

Ilene and Ted had been dating for six months when she was told her job was being "phased out." Ilene, who was 59 years old, had taught history for the local community college for over ten years. She loved her job and her students loved her. But the college was hard hit by budget cuts and it would be much cheaper to hire a part-time teacher, fresh out of college, who wouldn't expect the level of pay and benefits which Ilene took home.

The forced retirement hit Ilene hard. She was bewildered and hurt by her change of status. Most of her friends were colleagues and staff at the college so she lost both her social network and her structure.

Up until her retirement, she was enjoying a pleasant dating relationship with Ted, a 63-year-old real estate agent who was often so busy that Ilene wouldn't see him until late on Saturday night, after he was finally done showing houses and meeting with clients.

But with all this new time on her hands, Ilene began demanding more of Ted's time and attention. He couldn't give any more to the relationship, especially because it was spring, his busiest time in the real estate market. Ilene didn't want to lose Ted but she was beginning to feel she needed more than he could currently give.

Retirement can be a great time of expansion and relaxation for a dating couple. But it can also be a source of stress, especially if both members of the couple are on different timetables.

Retirement often affects the way you feel about yourself. If you enjoyed or identified with your work, you may feel a loss of identity. A work place provides many benefits including a sense of competence, structure, a social network, and usually a higher income.

With retirement, your income usually diminishes. Your time is unstructured, perhaps stretching ahead in endless empty hours. And your sense of self changes too. It's easy to feel lost, bored, or depressed when your established routine disappears.

That's the negative side. Retirement can also be a joy and a relief. A chance to do things you've put off for years. A time to relax, free from schedules and obligations.

No matter how you view this lifestyle change, it's an important transition and you'll need time to adjust. Will you continue to work part-time? Have you considered retraining for a new career? Research has shown that the longer you participate in socially engaging and productive activities the better your health and longevity.

You'll want to develop a balanced social portfolio in addition to considering your finances. In 1779, essayist Samuel Johnson, age 70, gave this timeless advice to his friend James Boswell: "If you are idle, be not solitary; if you are solitary, be not idle."

You can't always plan for the end of employment. Jobs can be lost, companies fold. You may decide to take retirement early, rather than look for a new job. If you're dating someone who is still in the work force, this change will affect your relationship.

If you're already dating but not a couple, you might want to take a break. There's nothing wrong with asking for "time off." Just explain you need to adjust to your new life and don't want to burden your companion with the stresses you're experiencing.

If Ilene had done this instead of pestering Ted for more attention, they might still be together. Instead, he ended the relationship, tired of her constant reproaches when he wasn't available to fill up the empty spaces in her life. For her part, Ilene realized Ted was a fine companion while her work was the center of life, but they really didn't have many common interests. She set about creating a satisfying life for herself, designed around her interests which included travel and photography. On a photographic tour of Italy, she met a widower who was able to share both her interests and her time.

Family matters

Spending time as a couple with your families can be difficult, considering all of the emotional history and family dynamics involved. Patterns are set. Traditions are established. Family stories have become legends that are repeated over holiday dinners. Everyone laughs at the story of what Uncle Joe said to Aunt Sally when he found the cockroach in his cake. Except your date.

Trying to integrate the person you're dating into your family's social life can prove challenging. Your grown children can set up obstacles even an Olympic hurdler would stumble over. They're sad your previous mate is no longer there. Even if they know everyone was happier after the divorce, suddenly the vicious quarrels and nights of tears are forgotten, and they recall the sundered marriage with a romantic nostalgia.

If you're not the first girlfriend or boyfriend, it can be even worse. The children don't expect you to be around long, so they don't bother to get attached.

Even the most grown-up of grown-up children can regress to the level of five-year-olds around a parent's new partner. They want to be children, cared for and secure within a stable family structure. They don't want to become parents themselves, worried about how late Dad is coming home or if Mom is carrying a condom in her purse.

The situation is likely to be strained even if your date is a reasonable, respectable person but it can be far worse if you bring a much younger or disabled person or someone of another culture or race to the table.

Ryan was thirteen when his mother died. During the year after her death, he liked having his father to himself but he knew Ralph would eventually find a new girlfriend.

When Karen showed up for dinner, Ryan

liked her. She didn't talk down to him and seemed genuinely interested in his schoolwork and sports. But when his dad invited her to dinner a second time, Ryan began to get nervous.

With the clever intuition of an adolescent, Ryan mentioned his dad's previous girlfriend, a woman only a few years older than Ryan himself. He also warned Karen that the cake he had baked for dessert contained about a million calories, a not so subtle comment on the extra pounds Karen carried.

At this point, there wasn't much Karen could do. If she told Ryan his comments hurt her feelings, he would know he was successful in his plan to drive her away. It was Ralph's responsibility to step in and let his son know he wouldn't tolerate rudeness or attempts at manipulation.

Since Ralph wanted to continue dating Karen, he did have this discussion with his son. He also encouraged Karen to establish her own relationship with Ryan. Luckily both Ryan and Karen loved basketball so Karen bought tickets to the Sonics games and invited Ryan along. It was a chance for them to bond and Ralph hoped it worked as he wanted to have a committed relationship with Karen.

It's hard to introduce a casual date into the family, so hold off on invitations to family gatherings until you've made the transition to being a couple. If your children want to meet your date, say something like, "Jackie and I are still getting to know each other. She's a nice woman, but I want to be sure things will work out before introducing her to my family. Be patient. I want to do what's best for all of us."

Sometimes adolescent-child issues can be a bit more malignant. My friend, Veronica, had a daughter who disliked every man whom mother dated. When Veronica invited Alan over for dinner, she warned her daughter that Alan had a seizure disorder. Sudden loud noises would make his eyes blink rapidly, his right arm twitch and cause a sense of temporary disorientation. As Veronica was dishing out the soup, her daughter let out a hair-raising shriek, then started giggling when Alan startled and began blinking. Veronica sent her daughter to her room but it was too late. Alan didn't stay for the main course.

When you're ready to introduce your date to your family, it is your responsibility to smooth the way.

My friend Erin had a hard time feeling comfortable with Lars' Scandinavian family. At first, it was fine since Lars enjoyed showing her off and his family, though never effusive, kept telling her they were glad she was "part of Lars' life." But after a year of dating, she expected to get more involved in family activities and that wasn't happening.

In Erin's large, extended Irish-American family (unfortunately left behind on the East Coast), the women of the family called each other on the phone frequently and got together informally. But this didn't happen in Lars' clan. She was included in formal family events — holiday dinners and birthday parties but that was all. They were never rude or impolite, they just acted like she wasn't there.

So Erin decided to be proactive. She called each of the women in the family and told them she wanted to be included in more activities. They were cool but agreeable; still no extra invitations came her way. Finally, because she was moving towards a committed relationship with Lars, she asked him for help. Lars spoke to various members of his family but no changes occurred.

It took a while before Erin realized Lars' family was not being deliberately rude. They were just reserved people who did not express their feelings easily, especially not towards newcomers. By recognizing the difference between their cultural values and the ones she grew up with, she was able to let go of her disappointment and continue to enjoy her occasional involvement with Lars' relatives.

Family matters can increase the complexity of the relationship between men and women of any age. If you prepare for problems, you're one step ahead. Be ready for difficulty but notice the rewards as well.

- Your children of any age can be unpleasant. You may be warned your date "looks like an old man" or is "out to get everything you've worked for your entire life." Statements like these can be gently put aside with, "I know it may be hard for you to see me dating. I'm going to make my own choice and, if it doesn't work out, I will move on."
- Your children may feel betrayed if you begin dating after losing your partner to death. "Mom's gone for only two years. How can you forget her so easily? Wasn't she good enough for you?" Children don't want to see a parent replaced. Yet they should accept your right to continue

life with a companion. Address this with something like, "I loved your mom a great deal and we had a lot of happy years together. She showed me how good it is to have a partner. I'll never forget her and no one will replace her, but I'm lonely and want to have someone to share things with." Don't add, "It's what I think she would want me to do" unless you got this statement in writing and notarized before your spouse's death. Suppose your wife told your children without your knowledge, "I hope he's struck down dead if he ever looks at another woman after I'm gone." Limit your explanations to what you yourself can confirm.

- Begin socializing with each other's friends and family at a slow pace. Allow time to ease into the other's social life. It's difficult to be the new person in a long-standing group. Try to arrange for smaller get-togethers; introduce your date to your community in a setting that's more quiet and intimate.
- Allow your friends and family to express their concerns. They may be unhappy with your choice of a date or just distressed at the idea of you having a new sexual relationship. Thank them for their

331

concern and say something like this. "I know you have my interest at heart. But for now, I've chosen to be with this man and I want to do things my own way and in my own time. I'll let you know how things are going." And do keep everyone informed about your status. Personal details are unnecessary but you can comfortably say that "things are going well" or "we're seeing a lot of each other" or "we're in a rough patch now and trying to work it out."

- Don't gush over your new-found love. Limit your hand-holding. Don't fondle each other in public. No sly asides about your sexual adventures. Assume your friends and family need time to adjust and might have trouble seeing your new love take the place of your last.

To conclude

Relationships evolve naturally. This chapter gives you some ideas of how to cope with problems and issues that might arise as you move toward a committed relationship.

If you can't navigate through these troubled waters with this partner, don't fret over what happened. No one is perfect. You will make mistakes. So will the people you date.

But I know, from my experience, and from observing my friends and clients, that you can succeed. You can find someone who will love you for who you are.

✦ 10 ✦

Breaking Up

Martha, a nurse in her mid-fifties, met Robert through an Internet dating service for music-lovers. He was a Harvard graduate with a Boston law practice, she worked at a hospital in Portland, but they both loved classical music. They corresponded by e-mail and spent hours on the phone before finally meeting in person.

Martha was impressed by his good looks: Robert was tall, athletic and silver-haired. He didn't seem to mind the few extra pounds she carried. Their cross-county visits were full of electricity. In Boston, they took strolls by the river, dined out a lot and had fabulous sex.

When Robert asked her to move in with him, Martha was nervous. Although she felt she had exhausted all her opportunities for romance on the West Coast, she was reluctant to leave her family, friends and good job. But she just couldn't let this chance of a lifetime slip away.

Living with Robert was very different from dating him. He had barely any furniture in his apartment because his ex-wife had taken all of it when she moved out. Martha learned that Robert's law practice was failing when his phone was cut off. And Robert was irritable and critical, constantly correcting her grammar.

She started thinking about breaking up. But she didn't think she could deal with the pain. And what if she was making a big mistake? What if Robert was her last chance at love?

Nothing seems more agonizing than breaking up. In fact, the fear of that torment might keep you from looking for love in the first place.

Rejection hurts even after a single date. Losing the fantasy of love can be as hard as ending a relationship of many years. But doubts and disappointment can plague you even if you've been with your partner long enough to have your illusions replaced by bleak reality. You know the relationship is flawed, but you keep hoping it will change.

It's tough to say good-bye, even to the most unpromising connection. And it gets harder as you get older. A breakup means going from the familiar to the unknown, so you may settle for what's comfortable. Even the most disagreeable union seems better than no relationship at all. Worse still is the fear that you're making a mistake. Whether you are the one leaving or the one who is left, you're afraid no one else will ever find you sexy or fun.

One reason endings are so difficult is that most of us aren't given any guidance about how to negotiate them. Relationships are supposed to last forever, and so people are uncertain about how to wrench themselves away from a bad alliance without anger and conflict. While you can't avoid the pain that comes from any ending, you can learn to minimize it.

Breaking up is hard to do

Lisa, a slim, active 55-year-old college language teacher, was delighted when she started dating Bill, who taught philosophy classes at the same university. During their first three years together, they created a busy social life, revolving around long dinners that sparkled with good wine, good food and good conversation with mutual friends. They discussed buying a house together and retiring to Spain.

Then Lisa found out Bill was having an affair with his 30-year-old secretary. And it wasn't his first extracurricular activity. Bill admitted he had also slept with the wife of one of Lisa's colleagues, a woman he met at a conference, and their Realtor.

"Why? Why? Why?" Lisa asked him.

"I just love all women," Bill said. "They're such wonderful creatures. But if you don't want me to do this again, I won't."

Lisa didn't trust him. She knew if she were younger and felt more attractive she would leave. But she had built her future around Bill. Breaking up with him meant losing that dream.

Breaking up has special implications for older people:

- We are not as resilient. It takes a longer time to recover from emotional setbacks. As years increase, so does our reluctance to change. Fear of loneliness and dwindling prospects makes us loath to trade the familiar for the unknown.
- We have new doubts about ourselves. The first episode of impotence or the onset of vaginal dryness tarnishes our image as young and sexually functional. As losses increase, so does vulnerability.

We grasp the last love as if to save us from death.

- We know our options are dwindling. Despite our history of surviving breakups, beginning anew intimidates us. While younger people assume a steady selection of attractive men and women, with age, the pool of available singles shrinks.
- We are aware time is running out. We realize the next potential mate may be more decrepit, have shakier finances and bring worse family baggage . . . if there is a next one. As the rusted mechanism of the biological clock grinds toward a halt, we are more inclined to stay in a miserable relationship.
- We are emotionally invested. We want to explore every possible way to make the boat seaworthy before jumping ship.
- We are ambivalent. We don't want to hold on but we are petrified of letting go. Ambivalence often arises from unresolved childhood issues. Even with introspection or extensive psychotherapy, we can't fully rewrite our scripts. Finding an explanation for a neurotic attachment does not make it easier to relinquish.
- We are needier. Dependency, problematic at any age, can increase as we age. We fear living alone and dying a solitary

death. Dependency is often distributed unequally in a relationship. The mate who wants more attention and assurance is inevitably the least powerful.

Yet, aging also brings advantages. We are wiser. With time, our judgment improves and our self-image has grown more dignified. We are less tolerant of quirks, insults and inappropriate behavior. We are no longer amused by destructive traits. In addition, we've survived breakups before — we know where to turn for solace and comfort. The sense that time is running out may even encourage us to hasten the end of a bad relationship. With luck, experience gives us strength to walk away from poor choices.

Why relationships end

Dating provides a period of discovery lasting weeks or even years. At any time along the way one or both can decide it's best to move on.

Some relationships seem unworkable to the participants as well as to observers, yet they manage to endure through endless cycles of frustration, doubt, conflict and reconciliation. Other connections drift into subdued melancholy, without sufficient momentum to be either happy or over. Such a lukewarm pairing might go on for years until one or both of the partners decides to break the pattern.

Sometimes the blow comes from the outside. Ken was a 55-year-old appliance salesman who loved his work. He had been dating Sally, a retired school teacher, for six months and was planning to ask her to move in with him when he lost his job. The company where he had worked for 30 years forced him to retire, replacing him with a younger and less experienced man.

Even worse was Sally's reaction. She had a history of going out with men who wanted her to support them. When Ken sank into a depression and stayed at home for several weeks watching TV and nursing his bruised ego, Sally worried history was repeating itself and declared she wouldn't go on. A romance that might have flourished under ideal conditions could not weather a crisis.

If you feel your relationship is questionable, take a step back and look at your connection from a neutral perspective. Pretend you're an impartial third person assigned to assess the viability of the romance of a couple you hardly know. Are they well matched or do you see glaring problems? Do they seem compatible? Be honest.

You may find yourself thinking about breaking up when you realize:

- You view life differently. Your mate is not adventurous. He likes stability; he feels limited by an aging body. You're still struggling with issues of identity, interested in new experiences and keeping your options open. Even though you may be close in age, you feel like a teen matched with a senior citizen.
- You need more emotional support. When life runs smoothly, or your partner needs reassurance, all goes well. But when your job is shaky, your friend dies and your daughter doesn't call for months, you need sympathy. Instead your partner snarls, "Get over it!" Although you know he is scared of his own vulnerability, you still deserve better.
- You're fed up with personality quirks. At 30, your demanding and manipulating companion was a charming challenge; at 60, the same behavior is tiresome. Character traits that were once appealing become less attractive as time passes.

341

- Circumstances change. Your partner re-
  tires, becomes ill or finds new interests.
  You see him in a different light and like
  him less. You simply don't want to continue.
- One of you changed. She helped you
  through your darkest days, but now you
  want a once-a-week date and not emotional life support. The rescuer role isn't
  enough to sustain the relationship.
- You don't like changes in your partner's
  personality. This isn't the same person
  you started dating. The positive first impression has faded. The bloom is off the
  rose.
- Tension and criticism are unbearable.
  You need some peace.
- You want space. You thought you wanted
  to be close, but too much intimacy is sti-
  fling.
- You can't imagine caring for him through
  a long and debilitating illness. You don't
  want to assume financial responsibility if
  the stock market heads south and her retirement evaporates.
- Your family can't stand him. Your children fight and even your pets hate each
  other. Holidays feel like funerals.
- There's no middle ground on finances.
  She lives on a fixed income and you like

to shop. Although his alimony is finished, his children still need a boost. When the pension comes, the former spouse gets the lion's share.

- The age difference feels weird. You speak different languages and spend too much time trying to fill the gap between Sinatra and Madonna. It was fun at first, but not any more.
- You want sex. You're sympathetic to his medicine's side effects or her menopausal miseries, but you're not satisfied with being "just friends" or infrequent fumbles in the dark.
- You want more than just sex. It's been great, but you never talk any more.
- You do talk but the conversation is dull. You no longer discuss your spiritual beliefs, your childhood dreams or your partner's attractions. Instead you talk about what vegetable to serve with dinner.
- You can't handle his jealousy. His self-pity and rage are making you miserable.
- You can't cope with infidelity. Your lover is bored and craves new partners. Sure, you understand this is his way of avoiding intimacy, but you don't have to accept it.
- You've got different goals. You want a

full-time companion, and she wants a Saturday night date. You need a partner; he needs a pet.

- You have no reason. You don't have to offer an explanation. No excuse is needed for not being in love.

When to call it quits

Deciding to end a romance involves powerful and subjective factors. To sort out the issues and begin the process, try to be as objective as possible. For starters:

- Create a score sheet with two column headings — reasons to stay and reasons to go.
- Weigh the factors in keeping with your own value system — not the values of your friends, relatives or society.
- Review your tally sheet and add to it when you think of something new.

Initiating a breakup can be as unpleasant as having someone break up with you. If you're the one ending it, you may dread the prospect of causing pain. You know how it feels to be rejected. You can't imagine doing this to someone else.

Some people stay in unfulfilling relationships because of this fear. Others endure years of dissatisfaction by living in a dream of nostalgia, remembering how good it was at the start. Others remain out of obligation.

It's your choice. But if your needs are no longer met and the relationship shows no promise, you need to consider ending it. Your health and happiness are important.

Your relationship may not be awful by any standards. It may look great to your friends, who envy you and ask if your partner has an available twin. Only you can judge if it's working. Remember you don't have to justify your feelings.

At first, Sylvia was charmed by her new boyfriend's love for cooking. Newly divorced and too busy running her flower shop to do much more than grab a burger after work, she appreciated Ron's home-cooked meals. Ron reorganized her kitchen cupboards, bought all sorts of fancy kitchen gadgets, and set out an elaborate dinner every night, complete with wine and candles. Her girlfriends and customers always wanted to hear about Ron's latest creation. But after a few months, Sylvia, ten pounds heavier from cream sauces and chocolate desserts, realized she was starving emotionally. "I'm tired of candles and wine every night," she said with a sigh. Like her conversations with Ron, the surface looked good but there was nothing underneath. She knew she was going to have to break up with Ron, even though her friends thought she was crazy.

If you've decided it's time to stop dating, timing is everything. Relationship decisions are best postponed when you're distracted by other life concerns. If you're battling depression or excessive drinking, if you're mourning the death of a friend or confronting a medical illness, these troubles should earn your attention before settling affairs of the heart.

But let's suppose the timing is right. You've sought advice from friends, tried couples' therapy and taken a break. Your life feels tortured rather than enhanced. Yearning for what is missing outweighs delight in what you have. There's no answer to your most pressing question, "Is this all there is?"

You've been updating your inventory for months. Even though the grounds to leave outweigh the reasons to stay, you may not be ready to break up. Don't worry. Cut yourself slack. By putting your concerns in writing, you're creating a foundation to bolster future resolve. Let me assure you that when the time feels right, you'll make the break.

Finally, after you've called it quits, re-read your list. You'll be reminded why breaking up was the best thing you ever did.

Being rejected

You're in a relationship where things are not quite right. Perhaps you're constantly quarreling about little things, or maybe, it's the fact you're no longer fighting that seems ominous. You wonder if maybe your partner is getting ready to call it quits. Think carefully. Are you secretly looking for a way out or is the end really in sight? Is your partner taking leave or are you re-acting out of fear?

Evan, a 60-year-old insurance broker, is in love with Linda. But he gets a knot in his stomach every time she mentions her best friend, John, or even John's home-town, Omaha. Evan asked Linda to give up her once-a-month dinners with John but she refused, although she invited him to join them. Evan is convinced Linda sees him as second-best. Linda says if he can't accept her lifelong friendship with John, he should leave. It's possible both Evan and Linda will use John as an excuse to end their relationship rather than face other issues that are making them uncomfortable.

Pay attention to signals. Ask questions. Remember: what you read in another's behavior may be a reflection of your own discontent. Watch out for these signs that might indicate your partner is losing interest.

- There are fewer phone calls and requests for dates. She hasn't called for weeks and, when you get her on the phone, she finds excuses to cut it short.
- Promises don't materialize. It's pardonable fluff to hear on a second date, "I'm going to buy an RV so we can retire and see the country." But if he says, "Let's go to the movies on Friday," then never mentions it again, that is cause for concern.
- Love talk subsides. You used to discuss how you'd waited a lifetime to find each other and how you'd spend the rest of your lives together. Now conversation centers on the local news and where to eat.
- Sex is less frequent and less intense. You haven't held hands or kissed for weeks.

- You feel bored. He looks bored. It's an effort to talk. You can't say what's on your mind because it's not nice to complain.
- You can't seem to find any convenient time to get together.
- There are no signs. The axe falls without warning. Don't blame yourself if you didn't see it coming. You're neither stupid nor blind. Some people are opaque and difficult to read, while others are masters at keeping secrets.

What's going on?

You might be wondering how your mate is feeling. Sure, you could ask what's going on. But perhaps you'd rather not know the truth. You might hear, "I don't find you attractive anymore." Unpleasant as it seems, it's better to be informed. Closing your eyes won't make the problem disappear.

Don't ask questions your partner can answer with yes or no. For example, "Are you thinking of ending it?" may result in a curt, "Of course not. What makes you think that?" Not only is the response unconvincing, it puts you on the defensive.

To get maximum information, ask open-ended questions. You might try:

- How do you think things have been going between us?
- Our relationship hasn't felt quite right for the past few weeks. What's on your mind?
- I've been giving some thought to what it's been like to be together. It feels as if we are at a crossroads. What do you think?

You may be the one who wants to detach, but can't bring yourself to say it. Remember the commandment, "Do unto others." If you are asked the above questions, have the courtesy to reply:

- No, this hasn't felt quite right for me. I'd like to talk about what I can do to feel better.
- I've been asking myself the same question. After a lot of consideration, I'm convinced our relationship is beyond repair. I have been thinking about ending it.

Postponing the inevitable

Changing how someone feels is next to impossible. If your partner wants out, consider how unwise it is to pressure her to stay. Even if you convince her to continue, she may remain for a while, but chances are you will be rejected again. Better to accept the ending with dignity and find someone new.

No matter how painful, take your partner at her word. Is there any other interpretation for, "I don't want to see you anymore?" Don't fool yourself into thinking she really means: "I want you to change and if you do I might love you."

If you really can't live without her, here are some strategies:

- Ask to take a break for a while. Although it's just as likely her resolve will harden, absence might make the heart grow fonder.
- Request a session with a couples' therapist. A skilled mediator might help you air complaints in a neutral setting.
- Ask if there is anything you can change. Hope for an answer within the realm of reality. Put in a request of your own — at least one item that she can change — so it doesn't seem one-sided.
- Go for therapy on your own and ask for a one-month grace period before calling it quits. You may decide the breakup is a good idea before the month is over.

There is no magic formula, instruction book, or therapy that can help you change the mind of another person. No matter how painful it seems at the time, take the words "It's over" as a blessing in disguise. You are free to find someone who will love you the way you deserve to be loved.

Feeling the loss

Whether you end the relationship, or are the one who is dumped, a breakup stirs up powerful emotions. Even after one date, a rejection might trigger a whirlwind of feelings. Expect any or all of the following:

- Fear. You can't imagine being alone. Being alone means failure.
- Guilt. You're guilty because you couldn't fulfill his dreams. Because she wasn't the answer to yours. You're guilty for what you said, what you neglected to say, spending too much time together, spending too much time apart, not going to the gym. Or you're guilty because you did go to the gym, got toned and now believe you can find someone better.
- Disillusion. Your expectations weren't met. The other person wasn't as nice, ro-

mantic or honest as you first thought.

- Disappointment. Sex will end. The absence of physical closeness is sad.
- Disbelief. "This can't be happening. Not again." The world feels upside down.
- Depression. Loving is the reason you live and being deprived of love takes away life's meaning. Your life seems gray and empty.
- Clairvoyance. Before the deed is done, you may be haunted by nightmares foretelling future misery. One of my clients dreamt she was driving her car when she lost control. Her passenger's arm was mangled and, after it was amputated, she had to take care of him. In real life, her boyfriend, who made his living as a pianist, was getting ready to end their relationship. Because she had repressed her hostility towards him, it came out in a dream. If he was damaged, no one else would want him and he'd be dependent on her forever.

Easing the pain

One way to lessen the grief of breaking up is to mourn in advance. This does not mean poring over personal ads or asking friends to arrange blind dates. It's not the right time to fantasize about your next lover or take a new one for a test run.

Instead, review what you've lost — the good and the bad. It's appropriate to feel melancholy as you think of parting. Imagine a future in which you're alone. Will you have pleasant memories or will you sigh from relief once the conflict is over? Think about the future. Even if you don't put your plans into action, you now know you have resources.

- Consider moving. If you've been living together or your place is charged with too many memories, inquire about rental options, even if you're not ready to sign a lease.
- Check newspaper ads and the Internet for classes and events.
- Line up support. Know who's available for talk and activities. Discuss plans with people you trust. Avoid those who mean well, but make you feel guilty or see your future as dismal.
- Arrange a trip with a friend but avoid romantic spots that will stir memories.

Let others know you're thinking about being on your own. Talking about plans makes them more real. Your discussions will help sharpen the focus on your future. Whether you follow through with these good intentions remains to be seen. At least you've identified your options.

Finding emotional support

Friends and family may try to be supportive. But in the long run, they may not be much help. When you were young, your peers were also going through relationships at a fast pace. Now your contemporaries are more likely to be settled, and your choices might trigger fears about the stability of their own unions.

Acquaintances may find it hard to sit silently on the sidelines and watch you suffer, especially while you're trying to decide what to do next. They will try to move the process along, convinced of their own objectivity. You may find their advice intrusive or impractical, but you don't want to ignore or insult them.

Here are some ways to respond to unsolicited advice:

- "Thanks for caring. I know you want the best for me. At this point I need you to listen. More than that isn't helpful. I hope that's okay, because our friendship is very important."

- "I'm wrestling with my own demons and they are personal. I have to fight them my own way and in my own time. Thanks for listening."
- "I'm struggling with my decision. In the long run I have to take responsibility for it. I don't want to blame anyone for a decision I make that's not my own. You can help me by letting me do this at my own pace and come to my own conclusions."

Don't ask, "What would you do in my place?" or "What do you think I should do?" You can confuse your friends if you ask for advice, then ignore it. This is your problem and another person's solution may be completely different from yours.

In the midst of a distressing breakup, it's easy to put your needs first and forget those of your friends. Revealing your anguish to an empathic listener is good medicine. It's a comfort to hear, "I know exactly how you feel." Events are less scary when you tell your story again and again. But in the throes of misery, you can easily bore even your most patient friend.

- If you've already called everyone in your phone book once, and you get the impression friends are starting to screen your calls, tell them how much it means to you when someone listens. Request a definite amount of time, for example, ten minutes. If your friend agrees, talk away, watch the clock and end on time. People won't feel trapped when they know there are limits to what you expect.
- Be prepared for a hostile response, "I knew all along he'd lose interest in someone your age." Jealousy, once suppressed, emerges with spite. Just reply, "This isn't what I need to hear now. Maybe we could be in touch later."
- Don't insult your friends by disregarding efforts to help. Everyone needs recognition. When they offer assistance, give them a task. By taking you to dinner or helping you houseclean, they feel useful and you benefit from their concern.
- You may be surprised by warmth from unexpected sources. When someone you barely know offers support, count your blessings and accept with grace. Some people are at their best feeling needed. Enjoy their support while you have it but

be ready for them to disappear when you feel better.
- Don't open your heart at random. You should know someone well before you share personal information, otherwise your words may return to haunt you.
- Preserve friendships by being sensitive to limitations. Pay attention to responses so you can gauge how much your listeners can tolerate.

How to prepare for a breakup

Planning the leave-taking may seem callous, yet it's too important to be left to chance. You'll feel better about yourself if you can approach this conclusion with kindness and dignity. While it might seem easier to force the other person to initiate the end, you don't want to be a manipulative coward. In the long run it doesn't matter who calls it quits.

Even if you've been treated poorly, don't stoop to a low level of behavior you'll later regret. Assume you both wanted a companion, but you're not the right fit.

Very few endings are tranquil. A breakup can be just as stormy after a first date as after a first year. Expect the worst, but be prepared to express your feelings and speak up for yourself.

Focus on what you feel and what needs weren't met. No criticism, no blame and no room for discussion. It can only muddy the waters if you say, "Things would be different if . . ." That suggests there's still room for improvement. If you wanted changes, you should have discussed that at an earlier stage.

Prepare for the ending by writing a script in advance. Use as few words as possible to indicate your feelings. Rehearse before the mirror. You might ask a friend to role-play different possible reactions. Be prepared for a range of responses: anger, disbelief, surprise, insults, relief.

Keep in mind your goal is to say goodbye. State your reasons and support them with minimal details. Do not criticize or complain.

Be willing to engage in some discussion but keep it brief. Listen to and validate the other person's concerns. Be tactful and sensitive, but leave no room for misunderstanding. Don't feel obligated to provide responses and solutions to the other person's problems.

What to say

- Don't start by saying: "The last thing I want to do is hurt you." This makes it sound like hurting is on your agenda. Do say: "This is difficult for me to say."
- Also don't start with: "I care deeply for you." You might get the response: "Then why are you dumping me?" Instead say, "I've looked at this from every possible perspective."
- Don't be nasty. Don't say: "We have a lot in common, only I don't think I can face going out with someone who looks so old." Do say: "We have a lot in common, only some things don't feel right."
- Express your wish to end in terms of your own feelings without accusing or complaining. The time is past for repair. "I just don't want to continue. I feel this isn't working out." No one can argue with how you feel.
- "We're just not a match" is a good phrase to end a dating relationship of any length. Point out differences. Be prepared to keep any discussion short. Otherwise you might wear out and cave in.
- Admit your own part in the failure. "I don't have what it takes to solve our problems." "I tried to change, but I know

it's not working." "I'm sorry I can't continue but I've done the best I can."

- If you're not attracted, keep the focus on yourself by saying, "I'm so short and I feel awkward going out with someone so tall." Height is easier to address than weight. You might say, "I'm not comfortable with someone so different from me." Keep the emphasis on your preferences.

- Age is a tough one. Say, "There needs to be a spark and it's not something you can force." Or, "I'm afraid of getting attached to a person who might die before me." Then you might hear, "You knew how old I was before we went out. I didn't age ten years overnight." You could say, "I know. I tried. It simply isn't working for me."

- You may hear, "Please tell me the reason. I can take it. It'll be really helpful to know." Don't be tempted. No one is really helped by hearing they look too old or act too stodgy. Again, emphasize your preferences. "It's just not working for me." Your goal is to end this smoothly, inflicting as little emotional trauma as possible.

- If you've decided to resume a long-term relationship with someone else, be truthful. Emphasize your role in the decision. Be clear your former heartthrob hasn't been plotting to snare you back all along. "My previous girlfriend has contacted me and I have decided to give it another chance. Things would have been different if you and I had met first. We have only a few weeks. She and I go back years."

- If you've met someone else, there is no way to be kind about it. You can mention you've met someone new but it's best to avoid the details. Keep the focus on the reasons your present relationship isn't working.

What not to say

- "Maybe we could remain friends." The timing is wrong. Maybe in six months; maybe never.
- If asked to reconsider, don't respond, "I'll think it over and get back to you." Don't prolong the pain. You will just have to deliver your message again.

Honesty is always best, but sometimes, to avoid insulting the other person, you might reframe your reluctance in terms of your own past.

Clare agreed to a blind date with a man

her friend described as a brilliant re-
searcher, a man with elegant style who
sometimes walked with a cane. Yet when
Fred showed up at her door he was leaning
heavily on two crutches, and had to use his
arms to swing his foot onto the gas pedal.
Yet he was insulted when she offered to
drive them both to the movies. When she
told him she was scared because she had
been in auto accidents in the past, he finally relinquished the driving role.

Fred told her he was recovering from a
neck injury but she guessed from a comment he made about volunteering for a
multiple sclerosis fund-raiser, that he had a
more serious condition. Yet when he asked
her for a second date, she was reluctant to
bring this up. Instead, she gave him the
story she also used for men who revealed
past addiction problems. She told him she
was still recovering from a past relationship with a man who had suffered from a
serious injury (or addiction) and she didn't
want to go through that pain again.

Choosing the right time

After making your decision, the sooner
you leave the better. Act before you collect

too many endearing photos and memories of blended-family dinners. The more experiences shared, the greater attachment you create and the harder it will be to end.

There is no convenient time to give bad news. Yet some times are better than others. Have compassion.

In this age of extended families and overlapping circles of friends, it is best to end before telling too many others of your plans.

Before a vacation or holiday may be best, if you can tolerate spending the time alone. You don't want two weeks on a romantic beach with a person you never want to see again.

It is kinder to end a long-distance relationship before a scheduled visit. Why put both of you through a charade? If you're the one who cancels at the last minute, offer to pay for the other person's ticket. Be gracious if you can afford it.

Finding the right place

Select a quiet, public place. Don't choose a setting that has romantic memories, like the restaurant where you first held hands. You need a place where you can have the quiet and privacy you need.

You might prefer delivering your news during a walk. For safety, avoid an isolated woods or deserted path. No matter how well you think you know the other person, you can't always predict the response. You don't want to be assaulted or lose control yourself.

If choosing between your place and hers, pick where you have the freedom to easily exit. It's hard to ask someone to leave who is unwilling to go.

If you want to return gifts, bring them with you or use the mail. If possible, remove your things in advance. You don't want to break the news while collecting your underwear.

Take your time

You have a plan. Tonight. At her apartment. Over the past two weeks you've been removing your books, your favorite sweater. You owed her twenty dollars and you paid her back yesterday. You've made a list of the items you want returned. You'd like to say your speech and go. You start. Your mouth feels like you've swallowed the Sahara. Instead of saying you don't want to see her again, you take a deep breath and ask if she wants to get a video.

It's okay. Really, it's okay. You need more time. You'll do it when you're ready and not a minute sooner. Don't beat yourself up.

How to handle resistance

Wouldn't it be great if you delivered your speech and your partner looked at you with a smile and said: "I'm so glad you said that. I've been feeling the same way and I'm grateful you put it into words."

Unfortunately you're more likely to get shock, anger, tears, or pleading. Some people may need time to absorb your words. Hours or days later, you may get a call asking for an explanation or an appeal to change your mind. Others might try to smooth things over or argue about the validity of your feelings.

Michael invited Arlene out for dinner at a local restaurant, intending to tell her of his decision to end their relationship. As soon as they ordered, Arlene started laying out her plan for the following Saturday. She wanted Michael to come with her to visit her grandchildren, then go on to the theater and then join her for dinner.

Michael said, "I've enjoyed the time we've spent together, only I don't think we should make plans for the future. This isn't working as well for me as it seems to be working for you."

Arlene was clearly shocked. "Why not? This is the best relationship I've had in years."

Michael pointed out that they had only known each other for three weeks. "Although I like you, I don't think it's going to work in the long run. I'd like to find a woman who enjoys sports. I have a lot of free time and I want to spend it fishing and cycling but I don't want to do those things alone. I know you have different interests."

Arlene looked wistful. "I could change. You could teach me to fish."

Michael smiled at her. "I really appreciate your willingness to do that. But it won't work for me. Our rhythms are different. It's like I'm waltzing and you're doing the rumba. You love social occasions and being around people. I'm into quieter, more solitary things. It just won't work for me."

Although Arlene kept offering to change, Michael acknowledged her comments with kindness while repeating his decision. By the end of the dinner, although she was visibly shaken, she had stopped trying to change his mind.

Like Michael, you may have to repeat your message over and over.

> *You:* "It's not working for me and I don't want to continue."
>
> *Response:* "Why can't we try again? I can change."
>
> *You:* "I know you mean well. But I'm past wanting to try. It's not working for me and I don't want to continue."
>
> *Response:* "You'd be losing the best thing you've ever had. You'll never find someone who cares about you as much as I do."
>
> *You:* "Well, that may be true, but I don't want to spend any more time on this relationship. It's just not working for me and I don't want to continue."
>
> *Response:* "Was it something I did?"
>
> *You:* "No, it's not one particular thing. I just don't want to continue."
>
> *Response:* "You told me you loved me. Why did you lie?"
>
> *You:* "I didn't lie. I meant it when I said it. Now my feelings have changed."

Some people won't take no for an answer. Sue dated Brad, a judge, for about six months before she decided to end it. He was a solid citizen: president of his Rotary Club and a volunteer for Big Brothers. The problem was his personal hygiene. He passed wind and belched without ever saying, "Excuse me." He snored. And his underwear was never clean.

Sue thought she could change his bad habits. She set a good example by excusing herself whenever she as much as sighed. She told him how a fictitious friend solved his snoring problem. She even offered to do his laundry since he stayed for weekends. Nothing worked.

Finally she called it off. When Brad asked why, she gave him a vague excuse: "It just isn't working out." Brad didn't accept her decision. He began deluging her with e-mails, calling two or three times a day, showing up at her house with flowers. Sue finally had to tell him she was going to get a restraining order if he didn't stop. That worked and she was finally free of the judge and his dirty underwear.

Other ways to break up

It's best to end face-to-face, especially if your relationship has developed any depth. It shows respect for the other person who will witness your conviction and concern. However if you've only gone out with someone a few times or the relationship has been unpleasant, you might want to minimize the grief. Consider these methods:

- Write. Compose your letter. Read it aloud to see how it sounds. Be honest but kind. Use a pen on classy stationery, not torn pages from a notebook. Put it in an envelope with no return address. This sends a clear message you want no reply. A letter is final. You will not get a chance to correct misperceptions and you'll never know how the other person responds.
- Phone. Prepare your script and be ready for the fallout. He might hang up, scream or try to keep you on line to prolong the misery. Expect to hear a litany of your bad qualities. There is nothing rude about hanging up. No person need listen to abuse. You've done the task you set out to do. Hearing a person get nasty will reinforce your decision.
- Voice mail. Leaving a message precludes

unpleasantness on the other end of the line. Write your script. Make the call. End by saying, "I prefer you not respond to this." If she won't honor your request, show your intent to end communications by silence.

- E-mail. If you have a history of e-mail communication and know your message will be read soon enough (that is before the next phone call or date), this method has advantages. It lacks drama, which is desirable in ending a short relationship. Compose your message carefully and then send it. If you get a response, read or delete it. Do not reply. People tire of being ignored and eventually move on.
- Fax. Send a fax only if you've communicated this way in the past. Otherwise, it's the height of bad taste.

Remember: you've had your chance all along to express anger and dissatisfaction. Saying good-bye should be just farewell. No last parting shots, please.

Dealing with the aftermath

There is no way to avoid hurting no matter who calls it quits. Our society promises that if we are smart and try hard, we can avoid all pain. That's simply not true. Loss and disappointment are part of life.

Depression can hit an older person with a vengeance. If you're sad or angry it is best to acknowledge it. Denying your feelings is dangerous. You may lower your standards and indulge in behaviors that will hurt you in the long run. Don't seek solace in drinking, spending unwisely or hurtling into a replacement romance.

As sadness and disappointment fade, you may be left with residual emptiness. As we age, we experience a deeper sense of isolation. If additional difficulties occur at the same time as the breakup, you may be more prone to depression.

Expect other changes to compound your sense of inner loss. You may receive fewer invitations, if you used to do things as a couple. Vacations and holidays now call for solo planning. Your finances may suffer, especially if you were sharing expenses; and you may spend more money on social activities and self-improvement programs. At times, you'll wonder if breaking up was a mistake.

Second chances

When loneliness hits, you may consider giving your relationship another try. You plead for one more coffee date, a session of lovemaking or a visit to a counselor. You promise to shut your ears to the things that used to annoy you, anything just to get back together.

Be aware that if you're the one begging for a second chance, your partner will now have the power in the relationship. Her unpleasant characteristics may accelerate. She's even later for dates. His grandchildren, fishing friends, and ex-wife's clogged drain take priority over your needs. There is an advantage to this experience. It will help you remember why you broke up in the first place.

Marvin was in love with a beautiful woman named Elaine. She liked to wear swirling gypsy clothing, never called when she promised, and was always late for dates. Sometimes she never showed up at all. After a while her behavior drove him crazy and he told her he was through. But after a few weeks of missing her vibrant presence in his life, he called and invited her out to dinner. This time, when Elaine showed up an hour late, wearing dirty clothes, Marvin saw her with the clarity of distance. "This gypsy needs to go to the Laundromat," he thought. That was the end of her spell. Marvin moved on and found an attractive and tidy woman his own age.

Never use breaking up as a threat. Make your decision and act on it. Perhaps you will end up reconciling but don't expect it. Looking back on past relationships which ended, you can probably see with the clarity of hindsight that you're better off as a result. Some day you'll look back at this breakup the same way.

Sometimes, if each partner realizes the loss is too much to bear, reconciliation is possible. You look back and think: "If I knew then what I know now, things would be different." What you did was based on who you were then. Now you have a chance to make amends. Negotiations can start the relationship on a different track. A second chance is possible.

Register your complaint and state what you want to be better. "I feel neglected when you're on the phone with your grand-children all the time. I'd like you to spend more time with me. Could we visit with them on vacation and leave Saturday nights for us?" Know your minimum compromise.

If you have not spoken openly about issues before the breakup, this is the time to start. As painful as it might seem, you've been given the gift of a second chance. There might not be another. Look for creative solutions.

My friend, Martha, has a rare success story about finding love a second time around. She first met Danny, a fellow history professor, at the University's Faculty Club, when she was 35 and he was 40. She'd had a bad marriage followed by several useless boyfriends and Danny swept her off her feet. But after about two months of romance, he announced he was leaving for Canada where he always spent the winter break. She didn't hear from him again for three weeks. No postcards and no souvenirs when he returned. She found this odd but they kept on dating. For his birthday she bought him a sweater and fixed a romantic dinner. He was spending the early evening with his younger brother but promised to call Martha as soon as he had dropped him off at their mother's house. It was eleven before he called Martha to tell her he was on his way. Martha told him to forget it. She drank the wine by herself and returned the sweater the next day. He never called her again and she saw him a few weeks later with his arm around the shoulder of an attractive graduate student.

Twenty years later, she ran into him at a history conference. She was then teaching at a small local college for much better pay. She couldn't believe he had the nerve to ask her out after the sour ending of their romance from two decades earlier. But she was curious about his life and agreed to meet him for dinner. That dinner led to another and soon they were dating. This time he did absolutely nothing wrong. He called when he said he would call, treated her with respect and kept every promise he made. What had changed? Through a series of vicissitudes, including a diagnosis of cancer, a fourth and difficult divorce and the death of his son, Danny had adopted a different attitude towards life. It took a while before Martha was able to trust him again but he eventually proved to her that people can and do change.

Moving on

It's happened. It's over. No matter who dealt the final blow, you're now facing the consequences. You must confront the process of recovery and the prospect of starting again. It feels impossible, yet I promise you life will resume.

Grieving any loss is obligatory. There is no way to rush the process. Expect good days and bad. Fortunately feelings stay at fever pitch for only so long and then lose their intensity. You will begin to notice the world, get pleasure from small things and get back to yourself again. Slowly.

Don't fall into the trap of reviewing the past. Don't obsess trying to figure out what went wrong. In trying to spot reasons for the breakup, you may be tempted to find a scapegoat. "It was my entire fault. If only I had listened to him more." Or "It was all her fault. All she could talk about was herself."

Unjust as it seems, blaming the other person is healthier than blaming yourself. Anger wards off the depression that arises when you turn your anger against yourself.

Here are some suggestions for taking care of yourself while you are recovering from a breakup:

- Minimize expectations. Give yourself time. Concentrate on the task for today: a favorite magazine, food, music, a movie, not being alone.

- Buy something. It's okay. As long as it won't put you in debt.
- Recall the telltale signs the relationship was in trouble. It took a lot of energy to ignore them or justify your partner's hurtful behavior. Now you can feel angry and relieved. Letty remembered how Andrew was never on time. He was always helping out his granddaughter or his buddy or his neighbor but was never available when she needed him.
- Reread your list of the relationship's pluses and minuses. You'll see how heavily the negatives outweighed what you liked.
- Read magazine articles, see movies and listen to country and western songs about what happens to faithless lovers. Fantasize a lot of mean, dirty tricks for revenge. Just don't do any of them.
- You'll want to call. Like an alcoholic wanting a drink, you'll struggle with overwhelming feelings. The phone pulls your hand like a magnet. But it doesn't work. You end up calling and feeling humiliated. He doesn't want to have coffee and he doesn't want to talk. He only wants you to leave him alone. At best he will tolerate a brief interchange; at worst he will tell you to stop calling. Suppose

you can't resist your urges? Don't worry. You'll get another chance. Keep in mind you will find other pleasurable activities once you are "sober."

- Forget dating for now. If you seek instant replacement for your lost partner, your chance of success is almost nonexistent. Or you'll find that in your desperation for company, you've acquired a new set of troubles. Wait. Don't shortchange yourself or another while you are grieving.

- Depression after a breakup can be profound and must be taken seriously. You can feel so sad you want to end your life. This is the time to seek help. Call your local suicide prevention hotline and follow the counselor's guidance. Such advisors are experienced with talking to people with problems like yours. Visit your hospital's walk-in services. They can help out by listening, perhaps provide some medicine to help you sleep through the night, start you on an anti-depressant or refer you to longer-term help.

- Now is a good time to consider therapy. It will help relieve your sadness, your anger, and your withered self-image. Take time finding a therapist. There are many out there, but you should find one you trust. Don't choose a counselor based on charisma and good marketing skills. Call the psychiatry department of your university hospital or a branch of a local professional organization for referral. It's safer than using the Yellow Pages.

- Look for aid in new places. Check the Internet, local weekly newspaper ads, community center, or church notices for support groups. Identify short-term groups for managing grief or abuse. If your relationship had an addictive quality, try a twelve-step group. Although alcohol may not be your issue, you'll find a kinship with others struggling to let go. Attending one group is not a lifetime commitment.

- Don't stalk. Don't call, then hang up just to hear her voice. Don't park your car near his house to see who visits. If you are tempted to behave this way, seek help from a mental health professional before you have to hire a lawyer. Harassment is against the law.

- Recovery may not be as difficult as you feared. You did your grieving in advance. You knew that your relationship wasn't working and imagined what it would be like to be alone. You recognized your mistakes and decided how to avoid repeating them. After a breather, you feel ready to move on.

Remember Martha who moved from Portland to Boston to live with her dream man, Robert, the silver-haired lawyer? It wasn't long before Martha became irritated with everything he did. He was always late, always broke and complained constantly. They tried couple's therapy but his ex-wife continued to be an issue.

After a while Martha began checking rental ads. She already had a good job and new friends in Boston, and it wasn't long before she found a great place to live. Six months after she moved in with Robert, she moved out. "Now Robert can chat all he wants with his ex," she says, "and I'm not paying his bills. I'll take real symphony tickets with my new girlfriends any day over my fantasy man."

⊰ 11 ⊱

The Final Word: Enjoy the Journey

Believe it or not, being single on a temporary basis can be a wonderful time in your life. Our culture tends to portray loners as people with serious personality disorders. But you can be single and simply bursting with great mental health. It's an outdated notion that being single is a shameful state. You're neither a failure nor a loser.

While you're searching for a new partner, you should make a full life for yourself, full of activities and people you care about. You'll feel better and it will shine thorough. As you meet new people, through shared social and recreational activities, you'll make new friends. This social life will be your launching pad. Think of it as your roots. Finding your mate is like adding foliage to the tree.

If you put everything on hold until you

find the right man or woman, others will sense that you're looking for someone to help you with creating a life style. This might appeal to a really controlling partner, but that's probably not who you want to meet. Also if you're obsessive about your search, other people will sense this and be put off by your desperation.

I'm not telling you that you shouldn't make every effort to find a companion. I'm just encouraging you to make the most of your single state. You'll become a more contented person in the process and much more amenable to love when your chance comes along.

If you learn to live in the present, perhaps through self-observation, therapy, or meditation, you'll stop responding to the old scripts of your childhood when you felt rejected or demeaned because of who you were. If you're at peace with yourself, you'll make a much better companion to another.

You'll be happier. You'll be more attractive. You'll have something substantial to share when the special person comes along. "Would you like to play chess? I just learned" or "Come bird watching with me!" are much more appealing statements than "I'm working on losing weight" or

"My children never call me." Activities you develop now are pastimes you can enjoy by yourself while your partner pursues his own interests.

Practice love until your special love comes along. Put your efforts into making friends and widening your social network. Permit yourself to be interested in those you wouldn't have previously chosen. Find an e-mail pal abroad and learn about a different culture. Love a pet and you'll have the joy of a furry creature without the ambivalence of human foibles. Take a class and learn a new craft or language and become part of the educational community. Help the homeless and give of yourself.

And just another word: There will come a time when won't be single. You have my word on that. But remember what it was like to be alone. Keep in touch with your friends who are still single. Be empathic. Be available. You may need your friend's support in the future, don't burn your bridges.

Be brave. Take chances. The second half of your life can be better than the first. Want love? Figure out how to enjoy life, enrich yourself and be loving and you'll find the person who is right for you.

Books & Articles
to Read

This book is just the beginning. It's a Guide, not a Bible. No one book can provide you with all the rules, the methods, the tricks, and the pathways to successful living and loving.

As I researched this book, I found bookstore and library shelves bursting with books on relationships. Most were directed to a younger audience. Some did address the needs of older readers. If this is the first book you're reading about dating at an older age, look at this as just a start. Other books will give you a different perspective. Some books address dating or sex alone; others cover a broader range of subjects and include these topics as part of their table of contents. Let me encourage you to explore what is available.

Read what you think you'll find helpful,

ignore the rest. Become an active participant in learning about relationships. You'll feel better about yourself if you approach the search for love as a learning process. The more knowledge you gain, the more likely you are to succeed in finding the person who is right for you.

Here are some books and articles I recommend:

Amador, Xavier and Kiersky, Judith. *Being Single in a Couples' World*. New York: Fireside, 1998.

Amodeo, John. *Authentic Heart: An Eightfold Path to Midlife Love*. New York: Wiley, 2001.

Arons, Katie. *Sexy at Any Size*. New York: Simon & Schuster, 1999.

Atwood, Nina. *Date Lines: Communications from "Hello" to "I Do" and Everything in Between*. New York: Henry Holt, 1998.

Aumiller, Gary S. and Goldfarb, Daniel A. *Red Flags! How to Know When You're Dating a Loser*. New York: Penguin, 1999.

Bakos, Susan Crain. "From lib to libido: how women are reinventing sex for grown-ups." *Modern Maturity* 42:5 (1999): 54–59.

Barbach, Lonnie and Geisinger, David L. *Going the Distance: Finding and Keeping Lifelong Love*. New York: Plume, 1993.

Block, Joel D. *Sex Over 50*. Paramus:Reward Books, 1999.

Brawasky, Sandee. *How to Meet Men as Smart as You*. New York: Fireside, 1994.

Brings, Felicia and Winter, Susan. *Older Men, Younger Women: New Options for Love and Romance*. Far Hills: New Horizon Press, 2000.

Browne, Joy. *Dating for Dummies*. Foster City: IGD Books, 1997.

Butler, Robert N. and Lewis, Myrna I. *The New Love and Sex After 60*. New York: Ballantine, 2002.

Cloud, Henry and Townsend, John. *Boundaries in Dating*. Grand Rapids: Zondervan, 2000.

Cohen, Gene D. *The creative age: Awakening human potential in the second half of life*. New York: Harper Collins Quill Paperback, 2001.

Edelstein, Linda. *The Art of Midlife: Courage and Creative Living for Women*. Westport: Bergin & Garvey, 1999.

Gray, John. *Mars and Venus Starting Over*. New York: HarperCollins, 1998.

Gray, John. *Mars and Venus On a Date*.

New York: HarperCollins, 1997.

Harrison, Barbara. *50+ and Looking for Love Online*. Freedom: The Crossing Press, 2000.

James, Muriel. *It's Never Too Late to Be Happy!: Reparenting Yourself for Happiness*. Sanger, CA: Quill Driver Books, 2002.

Kemp, Edith Ankersmit and Kemp, Jerrold E. *Older Couples: New Romances. Finding and Keeping Love in Later Life*. Berkeley: Celestial Arts, 2002.

Kreidman, Ellen. *Single No More: How and Where to Meet Your Perfect Mate*. Los Angeles: Renaissance Books, 1999.

Kuriansky, Judy. *The Complete Idiot's Guide to a Healthy Relationship*. New York: Alpha, 2002.

McKinlay, John B. "AARP/Modern Maturity Sexuality Study." *research.aarp.org/health/mmsexsurvey.html*. AARP, Washington, DC. <research.aarp.org>

Marshall, Max L. *The Re-Mating Game: Dating and Relating in Middle Life*. White Hall: Betterway, 1988.

Mater, Rick and Wing, Kathy. *Date to Win*. Hollywood: Laurel Canyon, 1994.

Mulrine, Anna. "Love.com." *U.S. News & World Report* 29 September 2003: 52–58.

Osing, Richard A. *Love at Midlife*. San Francisco: Rudi, 1998.

Page, Susan. *If I'm So Wonderful, Why Am I Single?* New York: Bantam, 1990.

Rowe, John W. and Kahn, Robert L. *Successful Aging*. New York: Dell, 1998.

Rosenthal, Saul H. *Sex Over 40*. New York: Putnam, 2000.

Sheehy, Gail. *Understanding Men's Passages*. New York: Random House, 1998.

Simpson, Eileen. *Late Love*. Boston: Houghton Mifflin, 1994.

Tessina, Tina. *The Unofficial Guide to Dating Again*. New York: Macmillan, 1998.

Tucker, Nina. *How Not to Stay Single After 40*. New York: Three Rivers Press, 2002.

Wanderer, Zev and Cabot, Tracy. *Letting Go*. New York: Dell, 1978.

Westheimer, Ruth. *Dr. Ruth's Sex After 50: Revving Up the Romance, Passion and Excitement*. Sanger, CA: Quill Driver Books, 2005.

Wolf, Sharyn. *Fifty Ways to Find a Lover*. Holbrook: Adams, 1992.

Young-Eisendrath, P. *Women and Desire*. New York: Harmony, 1999.

Zukerman, Rachelle. *Young at Heart: The Mature Woman's Guide to Finding and Keeping Romance*. Chicago: Contemporary Books, 2001.

Websites to Explore

The following sites are appealing because they provide easy access, respect for the user and a gentle approach.

- <u>SeniorDatingExchange.com</u>: This is a small, but promising site with members located throughout the country.
- <u>SeniorsCircle.com</u>: The opening images of happy, robust and gray-haired people smiling, jogging and talking on the phone provide immediate encouragement. The "Just Friends" category is a painless entry into the world of personal ads.
- <u>Datingfaces.com</u>: Established in January 2000, it has a database of 250,000 people of all ages, including a large number of members over 50. The site is grounded in the belief that common interests predict relationship longevity. It has a unique feature for creating a personal identity without revealing private infor-

mation. As a member, you can create an individual web page and visit other web pages. Or, after you complete the 81-item questionnaire, the computer will find your match(es). A member can choose to participate in real-time, online chats where privacy is maintained.

- Imatchup.com: This site with 2.5 million members reported in October 2004 that its number of users 55 and older was rising at a rate 30% faster than the general membership.

- FriendFinder.com: Has a large number of over-50 users. It offers narrow search categories, sports and international interests.

- SingleDating.com. This general site offers access to subscribers who are over 50. You can peruse ads for free. One drawback is the scant information shown — a headline, small picture, geographic location and 100 words describing physical characteristics, age and ethnic heritage. To respond to ads, you must join FriendFinder.com. While other sites, such as ConnectAt50Plus.com, sound promising, they ultimately bring you to FriendFinder.com.

- Several search engines have their own personal sites, such as easy-to-use

Go2Net.com and the more complicated Yahoo.com. Ads are posted by date placed, so you cannot know if ads at the end of the list are current. It appears there is no screening, as the site carries a number of sexually explicit requests. You must be willing to ignore the offensive and forge ahead to genuine possibilities. The "personals" option at Yahoo.com presents a large number of singles from which to choose. You can browse their profiles for free as well as post your own without cost but you must pay $20 a month to communicate with your choices. If you feel it will take a while to find your match, sign up for a year of service for $90. Also try this general directory offered by Yahoo where you'll find links to a dozen sites for personals: Dir.yahoo.com/Business and Economy/ Shopping and Services/Personals and Dating/Seniors/

- SeniorFriendfinder.com: Here you can do a state-specific search of thousands of members. As with many other sites, "men seeking women" far outnumber women searching for male companionship. Registration is free and also provides you with access to chat rooms.

- Matchnet.com: If you prefer a multimedia approach, you can post five photos and an audio voice-clip. You select your relationship criteria from long lists of prompts indicating ethnic background, religious preferences, educational achievement and other categories. The site lists support personnel and sends notifications when new members join. This site also provides links to nine additional dating sites including a site for gay and lesbians of all ages. Yes, there is a tenth site but you might bypass <u>CollegeLuv.com</u>. Besides matches in the U.S., you can also meet people from Germany, Canada, Israel, the United Kingdom and Australia.

- <u>Datemaker.com</u>: With its voice mail feature, you can hear your sweetie's voice on line.
- <u>Match.com</u>: This large and successful site for both dating and finding friends is a modern version of the computer matching services started in the late 1960s. You make your request and provide information including picture and biography. They also offer two additional features — both of which are worth a spin. You can try "Personality Matching," a feature that compares your personality with that of other singles and suggests the most compatible matches. Or you can

try "2-Way Matching," a feature that identifies matches who would like to meet someone like you. You and your potential date are contacted and, if you like what you read, you exchange e-mail. The site is committed to providing a safe community and forbids sexually explicit material.

- Udate.com: With 94,000 members over 50, this site is worth a spin, despite its irritating advertisements and scanty information.

- People2People.com: This site, like many others, is an affiliate of Match.com and offers the option of placing a condensed version of your online profile in the personal section of your local newspaper. Placing the ad is free. You're notified via e-mail of responses to your ad and you pay only to retrieve voice mail messages.

Some sites are useful even though they do not offer direct access to personal ads. Try:

- Dating.about.com: This interesting resource is an umbrella site of 700 specialized topics. Although unwieldy to use, the page of dating advice carries pertinent information for those over 50.

Some sites cater to specialized requests:

- AgelessLove.com: Dedicated to relationships with an age gap. One of the interesting features at this site is the Older Woman/Younger Man Community Forum for support for intergenerational dating.
- LargeAndLovely.com: A tasteful site for finding big men and women; but it has a limited over-50 membership.
- ConcernedSingles.com: An introduction service costing $60 a year; offers heady profiles touting intellectual prowess and political correctness.
- Many sites cater to religious interests. Matchmaker.com provides matches for members of the Church of the Latter Day Saints, while Match.com offers profiles of Buddhists, Hindus and followers of Islam.
- Other sites are specific for adherents of particular religions. ChristianSingles.com and CatholicSingles.com are appealing because they are free for users over 60. Jewish personals sites like Jdate.com and YID.com (Your Ideal Date) attract a fair number of users over 50.
- Goldenmatches.com: Connects "singles in the prime of life."

About the Author

Psychiatrist and author Sharon Romm, M.D. is a nationally-known therapist specializing in the matters of the heart. She is breaking new ground in the psychotherapy of couples and older adults.

After earning an M.D. from Boston University, Dr. Romm specialized as a plastic surgeon, practicing at Georgetown University. She then decided to focus on other aspects of patients' need to feel better about themselves. She trained in psychiatry at Harvard and now is on the faculty of the University of Washington. Over her career, Dr. Romm has received numerous awards for teaching and medical practice.

Dr. Romm is the former editor of *Medical Heritage*, author of *The Changing Face of Beauty* (Mosby, 1991), and *The Unwelcome Intruder: Freud's Struggle with Cancer* (Praeger, 1983).

She has also contributed a dozen chapters to books and edited six collaborative books, and published over 100 articles in professional journals and popular press, including *Vogue* and *The Washington Post.*

Dr. Romm brings years of experience helping people create successful relationships, teaching and leading groups, and showing compassion for the loneliness of others. She believes in her subject: Being over 50 means you are starting the best part of life, and with the right advice, everyone can find love and satisfaction.